Mind Fuck

Mind Fuck

The Mass Psychology of
Creeping Fascism

Neil Faulkner

Resistance Books

Neil Faulkner is a writer, political theorist, revolutionary activist, and leading member of Anti*Capitalist Resistance. His books include *A Radical History of the World* (Pluto, 2018), *A People's History of the Russian Revolution* (Pluto, 2017), *Creeping Fascism: what it is and how to fight it* (Public Reading Rooms, 2017), *System Crash: an activist guide to making revolution* (Resistance Books, 2021) and *Alienation, Spectacle and Revolution* (Resistance Books, 2021).

MIND FUCK

The Mass Psychology of Creeping Fascism

A Marxist-Freudian analysis

Neil Faulkner

Published 2022
Resistance Books, London
info@resistancebooks.org
www.resistancebooks.org

Cover design by Adam Di Chiara

ISBN: 978-0-902869-31-8 (print)
ISBN: 978-0-902869-30-1 (e-book)

CONTENTS

Introduction

Towards the end of Aldous Huxley's *Brave New World*, there is a scene in which the Savage addresses a crowd of Delta hospital workers and calls on them to revolt. 'Do you like being slaves?' he asks them. 'Don't you want to be free?' He then hurls the drugs they are rewarded with at the end of a day's work out of the window, shouting, 'Free! Free! You're free!' The Deltas howl in anguish and charge towards him in fury. He is saved only by the prompt arrival of the riot police.

The Savage is a young man born naturally on a reservation. He has educated himself reading an ancient copy of *The Complete Works of William Shakespeare*. Transported to 'civilisation', he arrives in a world of scientifically engineered people, cultivated in bottles on a production line, then conditioned for their respective social roles. Shakespeare is banned in this Brave New World because his plays are potentially destabilising in a perfect class society where everyone, from Alpha-Double-Pluses to Epsilon-Minuses, knows their place. As the Resident World Controller for Western Europe explains: 'The world's stable now. People are happy; they get what they want, and they never want what they can't get.'

Huxley wrote his dystopian classic at the beginning of the Great Depression as a wave of fascist irrationalism threatened to sweep away the foundations of contemporary civilisation. His central message was that 'sanity is impossible' in human affairs. Commenting on the novel in 1946, he was inclined to moderate the message – sanity was now possible but 'rather rare' – and he cited in vindication of his continuing pessimism 'the ruins of the gutted cities of Europe and Japan'.

We, too, live in a world threatened by a surge of fascist irrationalism. In collaboration with three colleagues, I have written at length about this elsewhere. I refer readers to *Creeping Fascism: what it is and how to fight it* for a detailed exposition. Here

I will simply bullet-point five key arguments that I believe have been confirmed since we published the first edition in 2017:

1. Fascism is the hyper-charging of a reactionary cocktail of ideas – nationalism, racism, misogyny, homophobia, authoritarianism, militarism – so as to create an active political force opposed to progressive movements and radical change.

2. Fascism is not a fixed state-of-being, but a fluid political process. It develops through interaction with other forces in the context of capitalist crisis and social breakdown. It cannot be defined by reference to a checklist; it has to be understood dialectically and historically.

3. The primary agent of fascist repression is the existing bourgeois state. The fascist party and fascist paramilitaries are always a means to an end: the takeover of the state and its transformation by a process of *gleichschaltung* (by which, through a mix of purges, intimidation, and indoctrination, state per-

sonnel are brought into line with the fascist programme).

4. Fascism is growing in the context of a rapid shift to the right in mainstream bourgeois politics. The liberal centre echoes right-wing arguments on the national interest, the migrant threat, the need for border controls, etc. The traditional right becomes more openly hostile to women's and LGBTQI+ rights, movements for racial justice, civil and democratic liberties, etc. Fascism grows in this ideological space.

5. The broad context for this shift to the right on the right is the compound crisis of world capitalism – a compound with economic, ecological, epidemiological, social, geopolitical-military, and political-cultural dimensions. The essence of modern fascism is the same as that of interwar fascism: it is a counter-revolutionary mass movement to defend the system against the threat of revolution from below by the working class, the oppressed, and the poor.

This general argument will not be further explored here. This book is not an update or revision of *Creeping Fascism*, but a supplement to it. I have written it partly because the psychological analysis in the first edition of *Creeping Fascism* I now regard as quite inadequate, and partly because the joint authors could not agree on the psychological analysis in the second edition and it was therefore cut entirely. This, though, leaves us with a serious lacuna. Let me explain.

Marxism starts with the whole, the totality of social relations, and it conceives of the world as a contradictory unity in motion. Each particular can be fully understood only in the context of the whole, and only as something fluid, in process, in a permanent state-of-becoming. We are therefore obliged to analyse what is happening in people's heads if we are to understand fully the social, political, and cultural disorder of our times.

We face a global upsurge of irrationalism: climate-change denial, anti-vaxx and anti-lockdown movements, far-right conspiracy theories, brazen lies about fake news and stolen elections, the demonisation of Islam and other imagined threats, an upsurge of violence against women and LGBTQI+ people, and much more. A growing number of those gulled by these far-right arguments are immune to fact-based evidence. Many display symptoms of psychotic rage. Some give clear expression to such in explosions of violence – from the loners who gun down worshippers at a mosque to the mobs who take part in a pogrom. Violence, indeed, is a central component of the fascist mindset. It may involve only a minority at the activist edge, but for them it can be central – a release of psychotic rage legitimised by fascist culture-wars directed against women, minorities, and progressives.

Psychology matters. For fascist irrationalism – the toxic cocktail of nationalism, racism, misogyny, and so on – to become a political force it must be internalised in millions of minds. Fascism must be understood not only as a social disease and political threat, but also as a psychological affliction. The disdain for psychoanalysis traditionally displayed by much of the left must therefore be rejected as ignorance and prejudice. It is no accident that while Trotsky and the Bolsheviks embraced psychoanalysis, the Stalinists banned it in favour of crude behaviourism and the Nazis burnt Sigmund Freud's books.

Fortunately, we have a strong tradition on which to draw. It includes Freudian-Marxist psychoanalysts such as Erich Fromm and Wilhelm Reich; other Marxists influenced by Freudian ideas such as Theodor Adorno and Herbert Marcuse; some of the more radical psychoanalysts and psychiatrists such as Karl Abraham, Sandor Ferenczi, Otto Rank, Karen Horney, and R. D. Laing; and various other social commentators whose work offers psychological insight such as Norman Brown, Guy Debord, Erving Goffman, and Christopher Lasch. Others might be mentioned; a full list of the influences on my thinking can be found in the bibliography at the end of this book.

What I offer here is a summary and an update, but organised as an integrated whole, and put in the context of the Marxist theory of alienation. This is one of the reasons for eschewing formal referencing: since my aim is to present a single argument, a grand synthesis, any attempt to provide footnotes would have been exceptionally clumsy.

The book is aimed at the general reader, but especially at progressive activists involved, one way or another, in the struggle against the authoritarian right, the global police state, and creeping fascism. The text is designed to be as accessible as possible. I assume no knowledge, either of Marxist or Freudian theory. I explain all technical terms and concepts. I aim to weave many complex ideas together to form what I hope is a clear, coherent, and compelling analysis.

The gist of the argument is: that the atomisation, alienation, and anomie of neoliberal society has given rise to a pandemic of extreme narcissistic individualism; that this has produced a distinctive narcissistic-authoritarian personality type characterised by fear of freedom and psychotic rage; and that this has provided contemporary political movements promoting nationalism, racism, misogyny, authoritarianism, militarism, fascism, and irrationalism with a mass psychological basis.

Chapter 1 explains and expands upon the Marxist theory of alienation, and argues that neoliberal capitalism and digitalised communication have brought the experience of alienation to a new intensity. Chapter 2 introduces the Freudian theory of libido, and draws upon radical psychoanalytical studies to suggest that this is best conceived as a primal psychic life-force. Chapter 3 defines the patriarchal-authoritarian personality that was the basis of interwar fascism, while Chapter 4 analyses the narcissistic-authoritarian personality characteristic of the present-day. Chapter 5 contrasts the different personality types that underpin the progressive and reactionary blocs into which our society is increasingly divided, and attempts to chart a way forwards for all of us who are determined to defeat modern fascism.

I must enter one caveat and one acknowledgement. The caveat is that the text makes many broad generalisations which tend to obscure important social and cultural differences; in particular, the focus is very much on the developed societies of the Global North, and even here the generalisations may be applicable to some groups but not others.

The acknowledgement is to Ian Parker, a practising psychoanalyst and revolutionary socialist based in Manchester, who read the whole text in draft and made a number of valuable critical comments, on all of which I have acted. I am nonetheless solely responsible for what follows. Those interested in Ian's ideas on radical psychoanalysis should read another little book in this series: *Radical Psychoanalysis and Anti-Capitalist Action.*

2

Alienation

Marx's most detailed exposition on alienation appeared in one of his earliest works, the *Economic and Philosophical Manuscripts* of 1844; but the concept remained intrinsic to his thinking throughout. It permeates *Capital*, his masterwork on the economics of the capitalist system, which he portrays as a monstrous mechanism of exploitation and accumulation in which human-beings are dominated by the products of their own labour – a dystopian vision similar to that depicted in artworks like Paul Kelpe's 'man and machines' paintings in the 1930s or in films like Fritz Lang's *Metropolis* (1927) and Charlie Chaplin's *Modern Times* (1936).

Marx identified four aspects of alienation. Workers, he argued, were alienated from a) the products of their labour; b) the materials, tools, and machines used in the production process; c) their fellow workers; and d) their 'species-being'.

This formulation is not ideal. It lacks historical depth, seems incomplete, and surely makes a category error with aspect (d). Alienation is a social experience which changes over time. It is not restricted to what is happening in the workplace. And alienation from species-being is not so much a fourth aspect as a consequence of the first three (plus others): it is, in effect, the whole of human alienation summed up.

So let us re-set. Marx's concept of species-being implies that humans have a set of basic characteristics and needs that define them as a species. Some Marxists have tried to deny this, arguing that there is no such thing as an immutable 'human nature'. This is obviously false. The most minimal acquaintance with archaeological and anthropological evidence proves it. Throughout the entire past of our species, humans a) have been social animals, b) have engaged in collective, cooperative, creative labour, and c) have created culture (which we can define as the entire ensemble of products and practices, from material artefacts like tools, clothing, and buildings to things like language, art, ritual, science, laws, literature, and so on).

Without this starting-point, Marx's concept of alienation becomes meaningless. Alienated from what, we would be obliged to ask? If humans had no species-being, no essential human nature, the Controllers of Brave New World would have had no need of bottled embryos and conditioning centres to provide themselves with a wholly compliant workforce.

Alienation arises historically. It is a product of class society, becoming more extreme over time, and reaching a peak of severity in our own epoch, that of neoliberal crisis capitalism in the early 21st century.

It has been argued that pre-class societies experienced alienation – from a natural world that was often dangerous and unyielding. I find this notion unhelpful. I think it confuses two quite different things. It is a bit like saying we are alienated from dearth, disease, and death. We are part of nature, we draw from it and contribute to it, we are dependent on it for our survival and well-being, and it is therefore the object of our labour. To describe a sustainable/repeatable relationship between nature and our species as a form of alienation seems to drain the latter concept of value.

I want to insist, therefore, that alienation is a social relationship peculiar to class society, and therefore to the last 5,000 or so years of human history. It began when ruling classes led by priests, warlords, and kings (the three roles often rolled into one) took control of the land and started creaming off surplus agricultural produce for their own use. This remained the dominant form of exploitation until relatively modern times.

Let us take a snapshot, viewing matters through the lens of our alienation perspective. Medieval peasants might be required to perform labour service and pay taxes (to the king), rents (to the landowner), and tithes (to the church). But they probably had their own plot of land, access to their own tools, and a measure of control over their own labour. Probably, too, they entered into various cooperative arrangements with their neighbours. Theirs was a partial alienation from nature, the land, and the products of their own labour –

all usurped by the ruling class – but something less acute than the alienation observed by Marx among the emerging industrial working-class of the mid 19th century.

Factories and slums

The factory system represented a step-change. The social position of independent craft-workers – like the English handloom weavers discussed by Marx in *Capital* – had been similar to that of the better-off peasants. They had retained a large measure of control over their labour, their tools, their products. But the dispossession of the common people – the eviction of peasants from the land and the ruin of craft-workers by cheap mass-production – was an essential precondition for the development of industrial capitalism. The need was for a mass of workers with neither means of production nor means of subsistence: a class that could be forced into the factories because it had nothing to sell but its labour-power and for whom the alternative was starvation.

This is our world – a world where the capitalist

class controls the workplaces, the machines, the raw materials, the labour process, the products, everything – a world in which most work becomes dull, repetitive, stressful, exhausting, and devoid of meaning – a world of alienated labour. We have only to consider the experiences of workers in, say, a Shenzhen electronics factory, a Dhaka clothing sweatshop, a Glasgow call centre, or an Amazon warehouse to grasp the enduring relevance of Marx's 1844 analysis.

Industrialism and urbanism are modernist twins. Most factories are located in cities and towns, but rapid, unplanned, under-resourced development has created 'urban jungles' of brick and concrete, tarmac and cars, garbage and pollution, slums and shanties; places where corporations, landlords, and hustlers prey upon the poor, and corrupt cops and gang lords murder with impunity.

While Marx was writing his *Economic and Philosophical Manuscripts*, his soon-to-be lifelong friend and collaborator Frederick Engels was conducting the first major sociological survey of industrial urbanism, published in 1845 as *The Condition of the Working Class in England*. Here was another kind of alienation, as people were torn from rural villages and sucked into a vortex of factory labour and urban slums; torn from a close relationship with nature and the cycle of the seasons, from the slower routines and gentle pastimes of agrarian life, from an existence more in harmony with species-being.

The pastoral world has been endlessly romanticised by writers and artists. The harsh realities of grinding labour in the fields, of feudal-type exploitation, of ignorance and superstition have been too-often glossed. But however contradictory the reality, a painting like Brueghal the Elder's *The Harvesters* (1565), a novel like Thomas Hardy's *Under the Greenwood Tree* (1872), or a childhood memoir like Laurie Lee's *Cider with Rosie* (1959) do not lie: they give indirect expression to the violence of the rupture represented by modern capitalist urbanism. So, too, in a different way do the magical forests of Shakespeare's romantic comedies: these are no mere fantasies, but draw on an ancient folk tradition that associated wild nature with human freedom.

Something else was also lost. For the displaced were transplanted from villages based on personal ties – rights, obligations, and expectations, hallowed by time and custom, according to which a community of familiars lived out their lives together – to a metropolis based on impersonal, instrumental, contractual relations mediated by the cash-nexus. The transition from feudalism to capitalism was not an unalloyed story of progress. Marx and Engels knew this well. It is one of the reasons that Marx loved Shakespeare, who lived through the transition and whose plays acquire so much of their power from the clash between a dying old world and an emerging new.

'All fixed, fast-frozen relations,' wrote Marx and Engels in *The Communist Manifesto* of 1848, 'with their train of ancient and venerable prejudices and opinions, are swept away, all new-formed ones become antiquated before they can ossify. All that is solid melts into air, all that is holy is profaned ...' Thus are human communities torn asunder, their component parts exploded into atoms and scattered across social space, leaving so many of us lonely in a crowd, friendless and powerless in the face of corporate power and implacable bureaucracy. This is the alienation depicted in Franz Kafka's novels *The Trial* (1925) and *The Castle* (1926) and in the Ken Loach films *Cathy Come Home* (1966) and *I, Daniel Blake* (2016).

This experience is now fully globalised. When Marx was writing, the industrial working class was a few million in a world of 1.25 billion people, the vast majority of whom lived and worked in the countryside. Today, more than half the world's population live in cities, and most of those still living in the countryside are landless wage-labourers or insecure dirt-farmers; the traditional peasantry is fast disappearing across the Global South. The layered alienation discussed above – in the workplaces, in urban living, in a society of impersonal, commodified, bureaucratised relationships – now dominates human experience.

Anomie

I want to interject a comment here about anomie. This concept was developed by the conservative sociologist Émile Durkheim, largely as a result of his detailed study of suicide rates, which, of course, can be taken as a measure of both social and mental distress. Anomie can be defined as a state of normlessness. One of the consequences of atomisation and alienation is the dissolution of the social frameworks within which positive norms and values develop – the norms and values upon which the individual's sense of identity, role, and self-respect to a large degree depend.

De-anchored, the isolated individual of modern society, the lonely soul of the neoliberal dystopia, finds herself in a moral vacuum. The wider world is a place of competition, exploitation, and impersonal, instrumental, 'what's-in-it-for-me' interactions. It is a place of bureaucratic indifference, of computer-generated responses, and of remote, unreachable, incomprehensible authority. It is a place devoid of socially affirmative norms and values – a place of anomie or normlessness.

Durkheim's sociology was a conscious bourgeois reaction to Marx. Most of it is shallow functionalism. The Durkheimian concept of anomie can be read as a weak alternative to the Marxist theory of alienation. I believe it has some value, however, so long as we take it as an amplification of Marx's conception, since there is no question that capitalism does indeed jettison people – and increasingly so – into a social wilderness devoid of moral framework.

A version of the concept of anomie underpins much modern analysis of neoliberal alienation. Mark Fisher discusses the relationship between 'terrifyingly unstable conditions' and rising levels of mental illness in *Capitalist Realism* (2009). He argues that 'post-Fordist' work patterns mean recurring social dislocation, lives full of flux and insecurity, a 'don't let yourself get attached' culture. This, he reasons, has elevated capitalism's 'invisible plague of psychiatric and affective disorders ... [to] a new level of acuteness'. He links this with what he calls the 'hedonistic depression' of youth, whose low attention spans, lack of intellectual engagement, and lethargic indifference give rise to an inner emptiness and an addiction to electronic images, music, gaming, social-media trivia, and other essentially passive time-fillers.

Competitiveness and consumerism

There are further layers of alienation to be considered. A ruthless, grasping, competitive individualism is written into capitalism's DNA. Not only are capitalists compelled to accumulate profit in a survival-of-the-fittest struggle to expand and innovate; so too are workers compelled to compete in an impersonal 'labour market' where they must sell their labour-power to earn their subsistence. And they must do so again and again, amid the relentless churn of capital accumulation, where 'all that is solid melts into air', ever insecure, ever wary of losing their jobs, ever looking over their shoulders at those willing to work for less. Here is another social corrosive.

Competitive individualism is fostered by family, school, workplace, and media. That is not because it is 'natural', but because capitalism requires it. Corporations seek to divide workers against each other so that they can drive down wages. But they also need them as consumers, so they seek to turn them in on themselves, away from wider sociability and engagement to a focus on privatised consumption. The system requires atomisation of both workers and consumers. The synthetic humans in Huxley's Brave New World are bred not only to be compliant workers, but also voracious consumers. As the World Controller explains: 'Industrial civilisation is only possible when there's no self-denial. Self-indulgence up to the very limits imposed by hygiene and economics. Otherwise the wheels stop turning.'

Large parts of the developed world risked producing a surfeit of consumer goods in the second half of the 20th century. Politicians heralded the end of want, a new age of abundance, a 'never-had-it-so-good' society of ever-rising living standards. Sociologists talked of 'the consumer society' and studied 'the affluent worker'.

The danger was that demand might flag once households had acquired the full set of consumer durables. How many cars, washing machines, and overcoats did anyone need? A crisis of overproduction threatened.

The solution was massive investment in marketing. By the 1960s, no less than one in six American workers was employed in sales. The sales effort involved branding, packaging, and advertising; special offers and hire-purchase deals; built-in obsolescence and breakdown; a constant churn of redesigns and upgrades; a social world pervaded by corporate messaging that buying this or that or something else was the way to be sexy, clever, healthy, cool, youthful, fashionable. Corporate marketing exploited status anxiety and fostered a competitive individualism focused on families, households, and 'appearances'. In the new consumer society of privatised households and personal advancement, to be was to have, and therefore to buy, to own stuff, to possess more and better than others.

Herbert Marcuse was among the most sophisticated observers of this new form of alienation. In *One-Dimensional Man* (1964), he analysed the way in which the system cultivated 'false needs' and a neurotic kind of consumption for its own sake, of things that were superfluous, that served no purpose except to fill a spiritual void. 'The products indoctrinate and manipulate,' he wrote; 'they promote a false consciousness which is immune against its falsehood.' The result was a society of flat, listless, comatose people, drugged by consumerism, devoid of creativity, drained of critical awareness; a society where 'the subject which is alienated is swallowed up by its alienated existence'.

Even when the post-war boom ended, the neoliberal counter-offensive began, and wealth was redirected upwards to the rich, the system found another way to keep the wheels turning: the permanent debt economy. Household debt has sustained consumption even as wages, benefits, and pensions have been cut. The average American is nowadays $100,000 in debt, the average Briton £60,000 in debt. Mortgages, hire-purchase contracts, student loans, credit-card debts, and payday loans are sources of profit in themselves but also maintain working-class consumption in an age of austerity cuts.

Spectacle and cyberspace

Guy Debord identified another layer of the ever-deepening alienation in *The Society of the Spectacle* (1967/94). 'The whole life of those societies in which modern conditions of production prevail,' he explained, 'presents itself as an immense accumulation of spectacles. All that was once directly lived has become mere representation.' Society had become 'a pseudo-world' of 'non-life', one 'mediated by images'. This was alienation taken to an exceptional extreme:

> The reigning economic system is founded on isolation; at the same time, it is a circular process designed to produce isolation. Isolation underpins technology, and technology isolates in its turn; all goods proposed by the spectacular system, from cars to televisions, also serve as weapons, for that system also strives to reinforce the isolation of 'the lonely crowd'.

This is a richly dialectical formulation. On the one hand, materiality itself is dissolved into mere image. On the other, the image serves to regenerate materiality – in the form of manic consumption – but one without meaning or purpose. 'The spectacle is capital accumulated to the point where it becomes image.'

This is a development of what Marx called 'commodity fetishism', but one which he could hardly have imagined. The replication of the spectacle by modern information technology is equally something that might have surprised Debord. Here is the way I described this in *Alienation, Spectacle, and Revolution* (2021):

Anything and everything can become spectacle. An infinite variety of images can be created with click-button speed. Images can be sent across the world in seconds. Billions of people act as transmitters. Billions of screens act as receivers.

The Roman ruling class used 'bread and circuses' to placate the Roman mob. The modern ruling class offers an endless succession of electronic spectacles – sporting championships, state ceremonies, celebrity weddings, commemorative events, international summits, music festivals, etc. They offer an ever-expanding range of instant-access, personally-selected, zero-effort electronic entertainment. They supply a constant drip-feed of electronic hoardings for every conceivable kind of consumer pap. They prey on neurotic unease, on low self-esteem, on the inner hollowness of alienated humanity. Frustrated aspirations – to be rich, beautiful, fashionable, elegant, sexy, clever, respected, successful, whatever – discover a catalogue of commodities to satisfy them.

Social media is also spectacular. Narcissistic self-exposures firecracker across the internet. Cereal-packet trivia clicks its way across cyberspace. FOMO-anxious addicts check their feeds, add their comments, make their shares – every hour, every ten minutes, every spare moment. Corporate algorithms read each click in a second and trigger a customised tweak to the individual user's flow of marketing, fake news, celebrity tittle-tattle, and other bullshit.

The internet becomes an immaterial world

of virtual lives constructed of electronic bric-a-brac; a world of totally immersive alienation where nothing is done, nothing is made, where no real human relations are formed, no practical action performed, where species-being reduces to zero.

bit harsh

I stand by all of this and would add this further comment: that social media have ratcheted up alienation from self to the nth degree. Numerous social commentators have discussed the masks that people are required to wear in class society, the way they must kow-tow to higher-ups, subscribe to corporate values, conform to bureaucratic norms, project an image of positivity, follow the dress code, and so on. The American sociologist Erving Goffman, writing in *The Presentation of Self in Everyday Life* (1959), described the way in which people were compelled to create and market a synthetic personality, to become social performers like actors on a stage, even to the point where this, the façade, is all that remains, so completely does the individual become the image.

Goffman was primarily concerned with the roles and performances imposed on the self by others. Now we have something more: roles and performances imposed on the self by the self, as it strives to conform to the algorithm-determined, click-baited churn of images on social media.

Is this not the ultimate alienation: when inner being is reduced to a performance prescribed by electronic images and mediated by corporate commodities; when people turn themselves into spectacles of consumption?

Digitalised dystopia

Even so, this is not the only way in which digitalised neoliberal capitalism has intensified alienation. Fifty years ago, many working-class communities were relatively geographically stable, being organised around local industries in towns or suburbs where people often lived out their entire lives and generation followed generation. In Britain, community was based on family and neighbourhood, pub and club, trade union and local Labour Party. Sociological studies reported on the closeness and solidarity of these 'traditional' working-class communities – in London's East End, in mining villages built around a local pit, or in old textile, steelmaking, or shipbuilding towns. Even newer industries like car-making involved elements of this. The biggest factory complexes employed relatively stable workforces of up to 40,000. Workplace union organisation was exceptionally strong, with high levels of wildcat strike action in rapid response to management attacks, led by shop stewards directly elected by the workers. Many 'white-collar' workers also became heavily unionised in the post-war period, with teachers, nurses, civil servants, local-government workers, and others involved in strike action. Strong labour movements, in short, represented a partial transcendence of alienation, a reassertion of human solidarity.

Forty years of neoliberalism have destroyed much of this. The decline of old industries, the more rapid turnover of capital, the lack of stable 'jobs-for-life' employment, and the deliberate smashing of labour organisation by union-busting managements, anti-union laws, and police violence have fragmented and precariatised the working class. The capitalist ideal – a subject class formed of atomised workers and consumers – has been substantially realised. The consequences are dire – management bullying, workplace stress, low pay, high debt, unaffordable housing, rising bills, a hollow existence of vacuous spectacles (celebrity culture, game shows, social-media trivia) and neurotic consumerism.

Our species-being – and therefore our mental health and wellbeing – requires us to engage in free, creative, collective labour; to have a practical relationship with nature, society, and the material world; to be active makers of our own culture; to be artisans, artists, scientists, and scholars. Instead, modern humanity experiences a multi-layered alienation, an inner hollowness, a deep unhappiness, for we are estranged from nature and the land, from free association with our fellows, from the productive process, from our real needs, from materiality itself, even from our real selves. We have become, to the very core of existence, artefacts of a vast mechanism of exploitation and accumulation, of forced labour and frenetic consumption, of electronic images.

We are not bred for labour and consumption like the inhabitants of Brave New World; but we have been rendered wooden, mechanical, automated, 'one-dimensional' by corporate power, bureaucratic control, state repression, and electronic conditioning; we have become the Betas, Gammas, Deltas, and Epsilons of globalised, financialised, digitalised neoliberal capitalism, each of us a tiny cog of labour and consumption in a vast mechanism of exploitation and accumulation in the interests of the super-rich.

Modern fascism grows in the psychic seedbed of this digitalised dystopia.

3

Libido

It is the essence of the world's greatest dramas. To watch Aeschylus' *Oresteia*, Sophocles' *Antigone*, or Shakespeare's *Hamlet* or *Macbeth* is to watch human-beings propelled to destruction – to death or madness – by a moral conflict so profound that it is beyond resolution. Should Orestes commit the most horrific of crimes – the murder of his mother – to avenge the murder of his father? Should Antigone defy the state and the rule of law to honour the obligations of kinship and give her outlaw brother proper burial? Little wonder that paralysis can afflict the tragic hero. Hamlet hesitates on the brink, his mind torn between melancholic doubt and a duty of vengeance. Macbeth experiences psychic implosion, driven to serial murder by ambition, but plagued by spectres of guilt. 'Will all great

Neptune's ocean wash this blood from my hand?'
he cries out in his anguish.

Both Marx and Freud made frequent reference
to Shakespeare. No wonder: for the essence of
Shakespearean tragedy is contradiction – both in
the social world and in the human mind.

As important in understanding the mass psychology of modern fascism as Marx's theory of
alienation is Freud's theory of libido. And just as I
have offered a lengthy, amended, and updated ac-
count of the former, I shall do the same with the
latter.

Until we have these two theoretical foundations in place, we will not be able to understand the
psychic wellsprings of the fascist mindset. I therefore crave the reader's forbearance. We may appear
to be embarked on a wide digression. But our des-
tination will be in mind throughout.

I have already made the general point that
Marxism starts with the whole, the totality of social relations, and it conceives of the world as a contradictory unity in motion. This Hegelian-Marxist
'dialectical' conception of social reality informed
the whole of Marx's analysis of economics, society,

and history, and it has remained the basis of all serious Marxist analysis ever since.

This method of analysis is the basis of Marxism's claim to scientific status – in contrast to various forms of bourgeois thought, where the approach is merely empirical (an accumulation of data), or the perspective is either static (a mere sociological snapshot), fragmented and partial (as in much mainstream historiography), or, worst of all, informed by political ideology (usually some version of conservatism or liberalism).

Much the same applies to psychology, where Freud can be considered the founder of a scientific approach to the understanding of the human mind, not least because he analysed the mental apparatus as an integrated whole.

But Freud was a middle-class Viennese liberal, and while often at pains to provide social context for mental disorder, and also increasingly interested in applying psychoanalytical insight to such social phenomena as religion, he never arrived at a satisfactory synthesis of the twin sciences of mind and society. Here we are obliged to attempt this, and we shall draw on the work of a wide range of radical psychoanalysts and social scientists as we do so. But we must begin with the foundation blocks provided by Freud himself.

Freud's masterwork was *The Interpretation of Dreams*, published in 1899. It is as fundamental to psychoanalysis as *The Origin of Species* (1859) is to evolutionary biology or *Capital* (1867) to economics. Central to the entire analysis is the dichotomy between the latent content of the dream (the dream-thoughts) and the manifest content of the dream (the dream-images). It is this dichotomy that gives dreams their peculiar, surreal, often nonsensical character, as if each of us had our own private night-time theatre of the absurd where anything goes.

To say that the dichotomy in question is the living heart of Freudian psychology would be no exaggeration. We shall review the matter in its two halves.

The unconscious

On one side, Freud places the Unconscious (though he sometimes, in later works, uses the term 'the Id' in a somewhat similar way). This can be thought of as the power-house of the mind, where all the basic desires and urges that provide the energy and motive forces of our mental apparatus are stored. So fundamental is it, Freud insists, that 'the Unconscious is the true psychical reality' – implying that everything else is a sort of mechanical superstructure that would be wholly inert without this power-plant.

The radioactive core of the power-plant comprises early memories of infantile impulses. Not only dreams but all normal human function (and dysfunction or mental disorder) turn out to be rooted in these infantile impulses; more precisely, to comprise desires or wishes arising from unconscious childhood memories, which may, in healthy people, achieve expression in affirmative relationships and life-enhancing activity, or, in unhealthy people, plagued by long-forgotten frustrations and prohibitions which cannot be sublimated and channelled, turn into anxiety, fear, and rage.

Children's impulses are, of course, raw and unmediated. Infants resent the father's interference with their special relationship with the mother and may even wish the father dead. (This is the famous 'Oedipus complex', though Freud considered it to be mainly a boy thing, which seems wrong, and also placed too much emphasis on a mental phenomenon that may have been especially prevalent in middle-class families in turn-of-the-century Vienna but was not necessarily so in other cultures.) Older infants resent the arrival of a new sibling, a rival for their mother's attention, and lash out at the intruder in the cot. Toddlers become frustrated by their lack of control, by restrictions on their freedom of action, by their inability to achieve immediate gratification of their desires, and the result is an intractable tantrum.

It would be easy to pile up examples drawn from the whole corpus of psychoanalytical studies, but this would be far beyond our purpose here. Suffice to say that these early impulses – so strongly imprinted on young minds still in formation – lie at the core of the Unconscious. They are never extinguished. They remain an indestructible mass of memories and impulses capable of erupting into renewed activity – that is, into an excitatory mental process seeking discharge – when some trigger is pulled. Infantile impulses are the mind's eternal revenants.

This is very similar to the Marxist idea that human culture is cumulative. Just as each stage in social development builds on all that has gone before, so each stage in mental development is premised on earlier memories and impulses.

What makes infantile impulses so potent is the fact that they are imprinted on a blank sheet and face no internal restraints. They are as yet unmediated by the rules of social life that govern adult behaviour. Instead, their operation is governed by 'the pleasure principle' – a primeval drive to instant satisfaction unimpeded by any moral framework.

So far we have described the power-house, but have yet to give a name to the power-source itself. Clearly, the two are conceptually distinct: the Unconscious is a repository of the desires and urges that drive our mental apparatus; whereas Freud uses the term 'libido' to define the actual psychic energy harboured there.

The desiring-machine

Libido has been caricatured as a crude 'sex drive' in much popular discussion, often in the context of an attempt to rubbish psychoanalysis as a whole; so we are obliged to define it carefully. It is a rigorously scientific concept supported by a great weight of empirical data and theoretical discussion. Despite this, like any other scientific matter, it is a matter of ongoing research and debate; and, indeed, the way in which Freud and his contemporaries handled the concept continued to evolve in the course of their work. What I offer here is a workaday definition informed by my reading of both the psychoanalytical literature and what I consider to be relevant historical, anthropological, cultural, and archaeological studies.

Freud, let us recall, describes the Unconscious as 'the true psychical reality' – the, as it were, fountain-house from which multiple streams of mental energy flow. His notion of libido seems correspondingly broad:

We have defined the concept of 'libido' as a quantitively variable force which could serve as a measure of processes and transformations occurring in the field of sexual excitation. We distinguish this libido in respect of its special origin from the energy which must be supposed to underlie mental processes in general, and we thus also attribute a qualitative character to it.

The caveat in the second sentence relates to Freud's theory of the instincts, for he identifies two or three in all: as well as the sex instinct, there is also the survival, self-preservation, or ego instinct; and in some of his later work he goes on to introduce the concept of the death or destruction instinct.

I have never found this convincing. I think Freud is guilty of a category error, by which I mean that he seems to be lumping together phenomena quite different in character. That we need to eat, drink, keep warm, find shelter, protect ourselves from danger, and so on are biological imperatives which depend on sensory and somatic stimuli, not on deep stores of psychic energy. As for the death instinct – a concept evolved by Freud in reaction to the horrors of the First World War – I cannot see this as anything other than a doomed attempt to 'psychologise' matters which should properly be explained sociologically and politically. I think libido stands alone as the basic psychic life-force.

This view is widely held. As I understand them, for example, it is what radical philosopher Gilles Deleuze and radical psychoanalyst Félix Guattari imply when they write of 'the desiring-machine' and 'the body without organs' in *Anti-Oedipus: capitalism and schizophrenia* (1972/2013). They see human desire – a primal psychic urge that is originally undifferentiated – at the root of all social activity.

Let us explore the implications of this bold claim. If libido is the basic psychic life-force, it is the source of all motive and action, everything that we do from copulating to creating works of art. What makes this possible is libido's almost infinite malleability, its capacity to be reconfigured in multiple complex ways, much as the electricity supplied by a national grid passes through millions of connections to enable everything from powering a household toaster to supplying a rail network. But just as electricity, whatever the job of work it is called upon to do, retains its essential character, so too does libido.

We must pursue this a little further. Freud lays special emphasis on genital sexuality as the most intense and direct expression of libido in human experience. Yet the rather bizarre nature of copulation – the concentration of excitation in the genitalia, the rhythmic motions ascending to climax, the culminating orgasmic discharge – are perhaps too readily taken for granted. For this, as Freud explained at great length in numerous learned papers, was far from being the original primary aim of libido.

On the contrary, he identified three distinct phases through which the sex drive developed during infancy – the oral-cannibalistic phase (in the first year of life), the sadistic-anal phase (first to third years), and the phallic phase (third to sixth years). The first two phases are characterised by narcissistic auto-erotism, where the child's own body remains the focus of excitation and pleasure;

the latter involves reorientation on others, typically the mother, father, or other carer, as libido becomes 'object-directed'.

But we are not yet at the root of the matter. Our view is still too narrow to grasp libido in all its majesty. Freud makes passing reference to the idea that something deeper may lie behind this sequence of infantile sexual development and its eventual culmination in adult genital sexuality. In his dream analysis, for example, he says the following:

A large number of dreams, often accompanied by anxiety and having as their content such subjects as passing through narrow spaces or being in water, are based upon fantasies of intra-uterine life, of existence in the womb, and of the act of birth... Dreams like this are birth dreams... In dreams, as in mythology, the delivery of a child from the uterine waters is commonly presented by distortion as the entry of the child into water; among many others, the birth of Adonis, Osiris, Moses, and Bacchus are well-known illustrations of this.

Freud did not pursue this line of thought. This was left to two close colleagues, Sandor Ferenczi and Otto Rank, and I want to share what I consider to be their absolutely seminal insight into the primal origin of libidinal impulses. Freud rated both of them very highly and often cited their work approvingly, though he never gave explicit endorsement to their theory of pre-genital libidinal organisation. Yet I think it essential to a proper understanding of libido and its relationship with alienation. And we are going to need our two foundation blocks – libido and alienation – aligned if we are to arrive at a joined-up, holistic, psychological-sociological theory of modern fascism.

The primal trauma

In *The Trauma of Birth* (1924/52), Rank argues that all humans experience a primal trauma at the moment of birth and a secondary trauma at the time of weaning. He contrasts the intra-uterine experience – dark, warm, wet, rhythmic, consistent – which imprints itself on the developing brain of the foetus with the abrupt and violent process of parturition by which the baby is suddenly jettisoned into a wholly alien external environment.

Unsurprisingly, the baby's subsequent behaviour is dominated by frantic attempts to heal the breach through the closest possible physical contact with the mother, most obviously in suckling in the warmth of the mother's arms; until, that is, the secondary trauma of weaning, which can only be experienced as a shocking rehearsal of the first.

Rank is unequivocal about the enduring psychological significance, arguing that 'the anxiety at birth forms the basis of every anxiety or fear', that 'every pleasure aims at the re-establishing of the intra-uterine primal pleasure', that 'sleep ... is a temporary return to the mother's womb', and that 'the birth trauma [is] a real substratum for all psycho-physiological connections and relations'. The libidinal impulse to reverse 'the expulsion from the womb, that primal paradise, which is sought for again and again, with unquenchable longing and in every possible way' becomes the very taproot of all human endeavour.

The primacy of the genitals in subsequent human sexual development is immediately comprehensible, for here of course lies the original locus of the birth trauma. Sandor Ferenczi's distinctive contribution to libidinal theory in *Thalassa: a theory of genitality* (1923/68) – warmly acknowledged by Rank – was to offer a detailed argument to the effect that genital sexuality was a secondary development. It was 'an attempt on the part of the Ego ... to return to the mother's womb, where there is no such painful disharmony between Ego and environment as characterises existence in the external world'. Copulation becomes 'the expression of the striving to return to the mother's womb', for 'the human being is dominated from the moment of birth onwards by a continuous regressive trend toward the re-establishment of the intra-uterine situation'.

In short, libido, reduced to its inner essence, is a striving for connection, for union, for a reversal of the violent sundering of parturition, for recovery of lost oneness with the mother, for a dissolution of the self in the whole.

At this point we can circle back to Freud. In his later theory of the instincts, he posited the existence of two, Eros, the life instinct, and Thanatos, the death instinct. The first, to my mind, is a reconfigured concept of libido, broadened in the way implicit in the work of Rank and Ferenczi. The second, as explained above, I find unconvincing, and I gain confidence in this judgement from the fact that Ferenczi has no difficulty subsuming what Freud wants as a separate instinct into libido/Eros: 'Death,' he writes, 'exhibits utero-regressive trends similar to those in sleep and coitus.'

This generic definition of libido/Eros – or, to repeat, what Deleuze and Guattari call 'the desiring-machine' – has played an important part in Marxist-Freudian analysis. It was the basis of Herbert Marcuse's *Eros and Civilisation* (1955), for example, which was a huge influence on the counter-cultural movements of the 1960s with its insistence that 'the fight for life, the fight for Eros, is the political fight'.

But I am not really in agreement with the central argument of Marcuse's book, so I will quote instead from Erich Fromm's *The Art of Loving* (1956/57). I will have more to say about Fromm below, so let me simply note here that I consider this book to be a transitional work, a curious mix of succinct, sharp, scientific treatise on the one hand and mystical self-help manual on the other, as the author evolved from the revolutionary radicalism of youth to the comfortable conformity of middle age. Be that as it may, I cannot fault this:

> When man is born ... he is thrown out of a situation which was definite ... into a situation which is indefinite, uncertain, and open... The experience of separateness arouses anxiety; it is, indeed, the source of all anxiety... The deepest need of man, then, is the need to overcome his separateness, to leave the prison of his aloneness... Man – of all ages and cultures – is confronted with the solution of one and the same question: the question of how to overcome separateness, how to achieve union, how to

transcend one's own individual life and find at-onement.

Other studies have revealed the traumatic effects of 'maternal deprivation' in subsequent infant development, and the way in which separation of the infant from the mother (or primary carer) gives rise to anxiety, loneliness, and unhappiness, creating the basis, now or later, for mental disorder. Psychiatrist John Bowlby published a major study of the problem for the World Health Organisation in 1951, *Maternal Care and Mental Health* (republished in a more popular format as *Child Care and the Growth of Love* in 1953). As he explained:

... what is believed to be essential for mental health is that an infant and young child should experience a warm, intimate, and continuous relationship with his mother (or mother-substitute – one person who steadily 'mothers' him) in which both find satisfaction and enjoyment. It is this complex, rich, rewarding relationship with the mother in early years, varied in countless ways by relations with the father and with the brothers and sisters, that child psychiatrists and many others now believe to underlie the development of character and mental health.

Much of great import follows from this. Our central argument is that libido, the psychic life-force, is in essence a primal striving for connection, belonging, and union; that our mental wellbeing, in infancy and throughout life, depends on what Bowlby called 'attachment'. We have here a psychological correlate for our basic species-character as social animals hard-wired for collaborative creative labour. We can explain the immense range of human endeavour in terms of this instinct, from the pursuit of romantic love to artistic creation, scientific invention, and academic research. Libido is the psychic basis of all culture and civilisation.

Does this statement seem odd? To explain it,

we must turn to the other side of the Freudian dichotomy with which we began this chapter.

The Ego

Freud contrasts the Unconscious (or the Id) with the Preconscious and Conscious (or the Ego). The Conscious is characterised by self-awareness. It is that part of the mind that receives sensory perceptions of the outside world, that engages in conscious thought processes, that draws on stores of knowledge and skill, that communicates with others, makes decisions, takes action. The Preconscious, on the other hand, works unseen. Though it is adjusted to the demands of everyday life – it conforms to 'the reality principle' – its operations are hidden from the Conscious. Its role is to manage a potentially fatal collision between primal libidinal impulses originating in the Unconscious and the requirements of the social order. On the one hand it must censor and prohibit that which is socially impermissible (a process known as 'repression'), and on the other redirect libidinal energy into behaviour that is socially conforming (a process known as 'sublimation').

The two processes are intimately connected, for libidinal energy, like any other kind of energy, can be redirected – in psychoanalytical terms, 're-cathected' – but it cannot be destroyed: it must go somewhere. On the one hand, the Ego represses infantile impulses and wishes that cannot be accommodated in normal social life – those that do not conform to the reality principle. Murderous jealousy of siblings, for example, is driven into the Id, whence it may occasionally emerge in disguise in the form of dreams or slips of the tongue, but where it otherwise remains imprisoned and forgotten. On the other hand, the Ego sublimates the libido invested in such infantile urges into more socially and culturally acceptable forms. Archaic sibling rivalry may, in this way, become the driver of an individual's later ambition for success, recognition, and fame.

A moment's thought will confirm that these functions of the Preconscious are indeed hidden from us. Forbidden impulses and associated unconscious memories are not accessible to the Conscious; they are cast down into the inaccessible depths of the Id. The wellsprings of our life choices and interests – what to study at university, what occupation to pursue, what hobbies to take up, why we are attracted to some people and not others, why we favour one identity or lifestyle over another, why we have a taste for certain types of music or art and not others – are not transparent to us. What is beyond doubt, however, is that a complex mechanism of repression and sublimation is at work. Were that not so, we would all be psychotics and society would collapse into dystopian chaos. The Preconscious is the stern, silent, shadowy gatekeeper of the individual mind, and therefore the mental guardian of the social and moral order.

The psychological development of the individual from birth to adulthood can be understood as the working through of the conflict between, on the one hand, the Unconscious, infantile impulses, and the pleasure principle and, on the other, the Preconscious, repression/sublimation, and the reality principle.

Freud himself paid particular attention to the

main stages of sexual development. He divided these, to repeat, into a) an oral-cannibalistic phase focused on breast-feeding, b) an anal-sadistic phase focused on defecation, and c) a phallic phase. Critical to the process is the gradual shift from 'auto-erotism', where the infant libido is inward-directed and experiences sensual pleasure as something self-contained within its own body, to 'object-love', where the libido becomes outward-directed and consciously seeks, and increasingly so, sensual pleasure through a physical relationship with others, first and foremost the mother (or main carer). (Note that Freud's scheme assumes the existence of *pre-genital* sexuality, and that implies that Rank and Ferenczi are right to insist on the primal significance of the birth trauma in the formation of libido.)

This, though, is to schematise and simplify a process which in practice is immensely complex and variable. A number of points must be made in this regard.

1. These stages – and various proposed sub-divisions of each – are somewhat arbitrary

analytical constructs designed to facilitate understanding. The process of sexual development to which they relate is, of course, continuous and seamless.

2. The psychic imprint of earlier stages is retained when each is superseded, finding expression in many aspects of sexual desire and behaviour, and also contributing to character formation more generally.

3. There is no single royal road to libidinal health: instead, there is infinite variety in human sexuality and character. Freud says of us that we are 'polymorphously diverse', that is, capable of achieving sexual satisfaction in many different ways.

4. These stages of sexual development, with their respective impulses and imprints, are, as mediated by the processes of repression and sublimation, the basis of character formation and cultural achievement. Libido economy – the way in which the psychic life-force is organised, managed, and directed – and the way in which the conflict between the pleasure principle and the reality princi-

ple is resolved – lies at the very heart of human existence.

5. The outcome, however, is not fixed. Human sexuality and character are subject to change as the individual moves through life. Karen Horney's concept of 'situational neurosis' is relevant here. She argues that neurosis can be triggered at any point by adverse social circumstances; and, moreover, that it can take a mass form where similar character types infect one another. What applies to neurosis applies equally to psychosis, and of course to human behaviour in general.

Let me underline this essential point. On the conflict between the Unconscious/Id and the pleasure principle on one side and the Preconscious/Ego and the reality principle on the other – and on the successful management of libidinal energy by the twin mechanisms of repression and sublimation – depends not only individual mental health and happiness, but also, in a very real sense, the whole of human civilisation and culture.

Neurosis and psychosis

The road to mental health is a rocky one. I quite like Fromm's way of describing the mature, balanced, healthy Ego as one whose whole existence is dominated by forms of giving, for this implies outward projection of libido, whether it is the moderately sublimated libido of romantic love, or the more thoroughly sublimated libido of the poet, the philosopher, or the physicist at their work. Allowing for the fact that he consistently uses 'love' to mean libido, this is what he says:

> Love is an activity, not a passive affect; it is a 'standing in', not a 'falling for'. In the more general way, the active character of love can be described by stating that love is primarily giving, not receiving... Giving is the highest expression of potency... What does one person give to another? He gives of himself, of the most precious he has ... he gives him of that which is alive in him; he gives him of his joy, of his interest, of his understanding, of his knowl-

edge, of his humour, of his sadness, of all expressions and manifestations of that which is alive in him.

Fromm then quotes Marx, who wrote in similar vein in the *Economic and Philosophical Manuscripts* of 1844, arguing that unalienated humanity exchanges 'love only for love', whereas alienation involves a failure to achieve reciprocal love, that is, to forge real human relationships, making love 'impotent' and 'a misfortune'. Marx's formulations were somewhat awkward, but his meaning was clear: alienation is overcome by human interaction and intimacy; the individual self is realised as part of the social collective. Fromm's outward-directed, self-projecting, giving libido supplies the psychological correlate of this.

Success in this endeavour – leading to mental health and social wellbeing – depends on circumstances. Freud – middle class, liberal not radical, a medical practitioner not a political activist – never achieved a real synthesis of psychology and sociology. Most psychoanalysts and psychiatrists today maintain this rupture: they are primarily concerned with individual mental health, and most therapeutic practice is narrowly focused on issues of personal 'maladjustment' and 'breakdown'.

This is not the place to discuss the way in which capitalism distorts psychological practice, turning what are really social problems into matters of personal illness, 'medicalising' forms of behaviour that are simply non-conformist, encouraging others that are plainly pathological. *One Flew Over the Cuckoo's Nest* – a novel published in 1962 that was turned into a film starring Jack Nicholson in 1975 – gives vivid expression to the way in which modern society 'psychologises' individual deviance. The Trump presidency, on the other hand, has demonstrated that pathological behaviour is no barrier to high political office in our decaying social order. So there is madness and madness – madness that is socially determined, madness that is nothing of the sort, and madness at the summits of society.

Here, however, our focus is on the relationship between alienation and libido in an increasingly oppressive social order; on the way in which interactions between individual psyche, conscious self, and conditioning by family, society, and social media have given rise to mass psychosis and created the psychological basis for modern fascism.

As soon as we concern ourselves with dysfunction, with mental and social disorder, we find that it involves a withdrawn, in-turned, self-obsessed, consuming libido; one which, at an unconscious level, regresses to an earlier, more infantile stage of psycho-sexual development, Freud's oral-cannibalistic or anal-sadistic stage, where strong elements of anti-social narcissism are present, as well as masochism and sadism, a desire to be dominated and a desire to dominate respectively (two attitudes which are, in fact, closely related psychologically and tend to occur together in the same individual).

Karen Horney, in *The Neurotic Personality of Our Time* (1937) and *New Ways in Psychoanalysis* (1939), argues – in explicit contradistinction to Freud – that no psychic disorder can be studied independently of the social context in which it arises, and that the form and prevalence of such disorder reflect changing social conditions. She stresses that all forms of anxiety – and therefore all forms of neurosis and psychosis – are rooted in dysfunctional relationships with others; that is, they are socially determined.

Neurosis involves involuntary behaviour of some sort that prevents effective social functioning. It is a defence mechanism against the anxiety (doubt, guilt, fear) associated with repressed infantile impulses. Male impotence, for example, might be triggered by over-identification of a female partner with the mother, activating a chain of mental connections anchored in unresolved incestuous wishes.

Psychosis, on the other hand, involves wholesale retreat from an unmanageable social reality into an alternative imaginary world that exists only in the head of the individual. Norman Bates, the psychopath in Alfred Hitchcock's chiller classic *Psycho* (1960), is a fictional example. Bates murdered his mother in a fit of incestuous rage when he found her in bed with her lover. Unable to come to terms with the crime of matricide, his mind protects itself by denying what has happened and constructing an alternative reality. He retains the corpse, looks after it as if still alive, sometimes dresses and speaks in role as his mother, and in this guise carries out the shocking shower-scene murder of a young woman to whom he is attracted.

Horney argues – correctly in my view – that the traditional distinction between the neuroses and the psychoses (each of which is divided into a series of sub-categories subject to endless debate and amendment) is over-drawn; that in fact the two broad forms of disorder, both rooted in anxiety, overlap, such that many individuals display both neurotic and psychotic symptoms.

More important is the way in which prevalent mental disorders reflect changing social conditions; or, as we might say in the present context, changing forms and intensities of alienation.

4

The patriarchal-authoritarian personality

We are now in a position to pose the central question: what sort of mental disorder gives rise to a fascist mindset? Or, more starkly, as Wilhelm Reich put it: 'Why do men fight *for* their servitude as stubbornly as though it were their salvation?'

I am going to offer a preliminary answer by looking at two Marxist-Freudian studies of inter-war fascism, Wilhelm Reich's *The Mass Psychology of Fascism* (1933/75) and Erich Fromm's *Escape from Freedom/Fear of Freedom* (1941/42).

The work of both degenerated in the post-war period. Reich extended Freud's theory of libido into the mystical notion of an all-pervasive cosmic 'orgone energy' and ended up conducting bizarre experiments with an 'orgone accumulator' of his own construction. Fromm slowly abandoned the hard science of radical psychoanalysis in favour of a rather superficial liberal-idealist psychology in keeping with his increasingly conformist politics. In both cases we are obliged to distinguish between their early and later work.

The young Reich summed up his view in these words: 'Fascist mentality is the mentality of the "little man" who is enslaved and craves authority and is at the same time rebellious.' He regarded the patriarchal-authoritarian family as both the crucible of this contradictory mindset and the model for the authoritarian-fascist state.

He considered an oppressive sexual morality – enforced mainly by the structures and strictures of the family – to be a feature of all class societies, partly due to preoccupation with private property, rights of inheritance, and therefore patriarchal control over the sexuality of women, and partly because psychic repression facilitated social control by making people insecure, neurotic, and thus malleable and submissive.

The basic mechanism at work here is, of course, repression of sexual desire leading to various neurotic complexes – lust/guilt about sex, fear/craving for authority, rebellion/conformity in social behaviour, and so on. Reich's explicit politicisation of this paradigm was a major theoretical advance. It is now clear, however, that the primary significance he gave to the patriarchal-authoritarian family – which he called 'political reaction's germ-cell' – was overstated. The more liberal-egalitarian family of the last half century (at least across much of the Global North) does not appear to have reduced society's capacity for political reaction in the way that Reich might have anticipated.

Erich Fromm's work is of assistance here. He took a broader view, looking not only at the minutiae of family structures and gender roles, but at the whole nexus of social-control mechanisms within which the family is embedded in class society. He argued that 'fear of freedom' is a generic human condition – at least in class society with its repressive social structures and sexual mores – such that the experience of freedom is liable to intensify feelings of anxiety and a concomitant craving for authority, order, certainty, and the sense of security these afford.

The deepest psychic root of this fear of freedom is the birth trauma – the single most searing experience of human existence: the abrupt, violent ejection of the infant from the warmth and security of the womb. The separation anxiety imprinted on the psyche at the moment of birth remains throughout life. It provides the blueprint for sexual desire, family intimacy, human sociability in general, the yearning to 'belong' and be 'valued', the desolation of loneliness. Whereas Reich's conception was of a rather specific guilt/authority neurosis, Fromm's was of a more generic separation/security neurosis.

Both insights are useful, and both can inform an understanding of the mass psychology of fascism. It can be thought of as an infantile flight from the anxiety generated by increased personal freedom, independence, creativity, and self-expression, towards some sort of substitute womb, or parent, or childhood family, as represented by a traditionally structured, morally repressive, patriarchal-authoritarian social order.

By this mechanism, a particular type of split personality is socially constructed. On the one hand, Reich argued, the individual develops a 'character armour', a set of traits which have a repressive function and give rise to 'biologic rigidity, incapacity for freedom, a mechanical-authoritarian view of life'. This, he continues, drawing on Freud's phasing of infantile sexual development, involves regression from the genital stage to an earlier anal, auto-erotic, narcissistic stage.

Genital sexuality, in which libido is projected towards others, seeking satisfaction in union with them, is object-focused and therefore the psychic basis of love, friendship, sociability, team-building, solidarity, compassion, and other forms of cooperative/consensual human interaction. Both anality and narcissism, on the other hand, are associated with a wide range of subject-focused disorders, from the obsessive compulsions of the anally-fixated to the excessive egotism and selfishness of the narcissistic personality.

Repression, rigidity, character armour: here is one of Reich's two foundation blocks of the fascist individual. Mysticism is the other. In his most blunt formulation, he writes that 'mysticism is nothing other than unconscious longing for orgasm'. His point is that the character armour of the repressive-authoritarian personality is a defence against unconscious impulses and wishes that continue to operate, seeking some form of overt expression and sublimated satisfaction. This was evident in interwar fascism's mystical elevation of symbols, rituals, rallies, leader-worship, and military glory, and in its spinning of fantasies from the concepts of race, nation, and folk-community. 'The Prussian military parades,' Reich explains,

betray all the characteristics of a mystical and mechanical man. Human mysticism, which thus represents the last traces of vitality, also became the fountainhead of mechanical sadism in Hitlerism. From the deepest sources of biologic functioning still remaining, the cry for 'freedom' wins through again and again, notwithstanding all the rigidity and enslavement... The various cries for freedom are as old as the ossification of the human plasma.

Not only does this provide us with an understanding at the level of individual psychology of the appeal of authoritarian leaders, restrictions on civil liberties, and repressive action against dissidents; it also leads to an understanding of the mass psychotic rage often unleashed by fascist movements.

The individual fascist desires freedom but fears it. The example of freedom, the possibility of it, in consequence evokes acute anxiety. This anxiety is libidinally-charged. Let us recall that libido is the life-force, the psychic energy that powers the mind, and, as the physicists have taught us, energy can be transferred but cannot be destroyed: the damned-up 'affect' has to go somewhere.

Psychotic rage

The success of others in realising their own freedom, creativity, and species-being can become envy, resentment, and rage. The socially marginal, the personally inadequate, the sexually insecure – people who in some way feel themselves to be 'losers' – are liable to vent against those who challenge the traditional authoritarian-hierarchal order on which their sense of security depends.

When fascism authorises attacks upon external targets – on migrants, Muslims, women, LGBTQI+ people, the disabled, racial minorities, socialists, liberals, etc – targets that may symbolise hidden fears of failure, rejection, emasculation – targets that may trigger deep-rooted anxiety complexes – the result can be explosions of psychotic rage.

Such rage, when canalised and politicised, often takes a collective form, passing like an electric current back and forth through the crowd, gathering force as it does so. This is the process Freud called 'the return of the repressed' – a surge of libidinal impulses from the psychic depths, which can, in certain circumstances, take the form of murderous violence.

A young Ho Chi Minh (later the leader of the Vietnamese national liberation struggle) watched a Ku Klux Klan lynching in the United States in 1924. This is how he described it:

Imagine a furious horde, fists clenched, eyes bloodshot, mouths foaming, yells, insults, curses... The horde is transported with the wild delight of a crime to be committed without risk...

Imagine in this human sea a flotsam of black flesh pushed about, beaten, trampled underfoot, torn, slashed, insulted, tossed hither and thither, bloodstained...

In a wave of hatred and bestiality, the lynchers drag the black man to a woods or public place. They tie him to a tree, pour kerosene over him, cover him with flammable material. While waiting for the fire to be kindled, they smash his teeth, one by one...

The black man is cooked, browned, burnt. But he deserves to die twice instead of once. He is therefore hanged, or more exactly, what is left of the corpse is hanged...

When everybody has had enough, the corpse is brought down. The rope is cut into small pieces which will be sold for three or five dollars each. Souvenirs and lucky charms are quarrelled over by the women...

We can draw a number of lessons from events like this. First, that psychotic hatred infects large numbers of ordinary people. Second, that it may, in certain circumstances, flare into murderous rage. Third, that such hatred and rage is infectious; that it is legitimised, magnified, hyper-charged by the crowd.

But, as the whole world knows following the Nazi genocide, fascism provides a framework not only for the bestial violence of the mob, but also for mass, industrialised, cold-blooded killing.

Of seminal relevance here is historian Christopher Browning's book *Ordinary Men: Reserve Police Battalion 101 and the Final Solution in Poland* (1992). This unit was deployed to Occupied Poland in June 1942 to take part in a 'special action'. Eighteen months later, at the end of its tour of duty, Reserve Police Battalion 101 had murdered 38,000 unarmed men, women, and children. They had also deported another 45,000 people to

Treblinka, an extermination camp, where an estimated 750,000 Jews were gassed during the Second World War.

The most notable thing about the men of Reserve Police Battalion 101, as Browning's title implies, was their ordinariness. They were not members of the SS. They were not even members of the *Wehrmacht* (the German Army). They were ordinary middle-aged men from Hamburg. Their average age was 39, many had families, most were unskilled or semi-skilled workers, a few were skilled workers, and a few lower middle class. Many were churchgoers. They had ended up as reserve policemen because they were too old for front-line military service but were not working in essential jobs.

Early on the morning of 13 July 1942, Reserve Police Battalion 101 arrived at the large Polish village of Jozefow. Founded in the early 18th century, it was home to 2,000 Jews. Following an address by their commanding officer, the policemen drove the villagers from their homes into the marketplace. Any who resisted or attempted to flee were shot on the spot. Able-bodied young men (about 400) were then separated and dispatched to work in the nearby down of Lublin. The remaining Jews were then loaded onto trucks and driven to a forest near the village. Once disembarked, they were taken in a succession of batches, one policeman per victim, to a clearing in the forest, where the entire batch was shot in the back of the neck on the squad leader's order.

A small minority of the policemen (10%) refused to kill at the outset and were assigned to other duties, and a further small minority (another 10%) refused at some point later during the unit's tour of duty to continue killing. But four out of five in this police battalion of 'ordinary men' continued killing to the end – giving an average of about 90 murders per man.

Browning identified three distinct groups within the unit. In addition to the refusers, there was a nucleus of enthusiastic killers who volunteered for the firing squads, and a majority group who followed orders but did not seek opportunities to kill and in some cases refrained from killing when not being observed by superiors. But the simple fact remains: some mix of indoctrination, demonisation of the Other, obedience to authority, socialisation to conform, career aspirations, and peer pressure combined to turn 400 everyday men into mass killers of defenceless men, women, and children.

We are bound to press the question: why are so many people prepared to obey the state when it orders them to commit murder; why, in particular, are they prepared to do this even in the light of overwhelming evidence from history that the state is an instrument of persecution, repression, violence, and genocide; why, in the light of this, are so many people unwilling to trust their own consciences and sense of humanity?

Several researchers addressed this question in post-war studies, among them the Frankfurt School Marxist Theodor Adorno, who worked with a team of researchers at Berkeley's Institute of Social Research. They set out to define 'the authoritarian, anti-democratic personality profile that makes a person susceptible to fascist propaganda'. The Berkeley researchers identified the following characteristics:

- Conventionalism: adherence to traditional values
- Authoritarian submission to in-group authority figures
- Authoritarian aggression against people who violate conventional values
- Opposition to subjectivity and imagination
- Superstition and stereotype; belief in individual fate; thinking in rigid categories
- Power and toughness: a concern with submission, domination, and assertion of strength
- Destructiveness and cynicism; hostility to human nature
- Projectivity: perception of the world as dangerous; a tendency to project unconscious impulses
- Sex: an overt concern with sexual practices

Other researchers have stressed that these are not fixed character traits, but inherent tendencies, such that a large proportion of the population shares them to some degree, and therefore, in certain circumstances, if these traits are validated and fostered by the state, the majority may become significantly and dangerously more authoritarian in attitude.

But is this still true in societies where the patriarchal-authoritarian family of the interwar period has given way to a more liberal-egalitarian family since?

The family cauldron

Let me start by commenting on how historically distinctive the modern, privatised, small-household nuclear family really is. We take it for granted because it dominates our social experience. But archaeological and anthropological evidence shows that pre-modern (i.e. pre-capitalist) families were not typically of this kind.

In the past, people tended to live in larger, extended-family groups, and often enough in households of more than one kin group. This remains the case in many parts of the less-developed world today, and even in the more-developed world, as recently as the mid 20th century many traditional working-class communities retained elements of this earlier family pattern. The small-household domestic unit is a social form peculiar to capitalism, especially late capitalism; and that is because this form is advantageous to capitalism in a number of ways. This is how we explained it in *Creeping Fascism*:

The family is one of the building-blocks of capitalist society. Though it has changed radically over time, especially in the last half century or so, the family remains essential to the low-cost maintenance, reproduction, and socialisation of the labour force. It is central to each of the following processes: satisfying the basic physical and emotional needs of workers; providing the money, time, and effort involved in rearing children; caring for the elderly and disabled; and supporting students, the unemployed, and other family dependants.

All these processes could be collectivised. Some are to a limited extent. But the expense when this is done amounts to a tax on the system and therefore becomes a target for right-wing attacks on 'profligate spending', 'the nanny state', 'welfare dependency', and so on. Better, from a capitalist perspective, that the working-class family should carry the burden than that the state should spend on nurseries, care homes, social services, and adequate grants, benefits, and pensions.

Collective provision would have another deleterious consequence for the system: it would sharply reduce privatised consumption and therefore economic demand. The individual family household is an exceptionally high-cost unit, each requiring a full array of home, car, furnishings, gadgets, clothing, food, heating, light, and so on. The family-centred frenzy to consume is, moreover, sustained by an anxious competitiveness among households fostered by a massive corporate sales-effort. Consumers are encouraged to shop for the products that will make them classy, affluent, fashionable, educated, and sexy; the message is that you – and your family – are what you

have. This all-pervasive social disease of alienated consumption is centred on the household.
Capitalism needs the family as a mass market.

The family has other advantages for the system: it is a mechanism of social and ideological
control. Its very existence means that society is
broken down into the smallest of atoms – family households – and that social life is therefore largely reduced to privatised consumption
and personal ambition. It is difficult to exag-
gerate the significance of this. Every problem
– earning a living, finding a home, paying the
bills, getting into university, accessing medical
care, and so on – becomes a problem of the individual and her family. Despite the fact that
all of these problems are socially determined
– employment opportunities, the affordability
of housing, charges for utilities, the cost of education, the availability of health services –
they are experienced as private matters. Thus
the family hard-wires privatised ways of think-

ing about collective matters into our consciousness.

It is this, as much as anything, that makes
the modern family an incubator of conformity
and conservatism. Many families are still
blighted by traditional patriarchal authority.
But even in relatively liberal households –
where parental roles are less gender-specific
and parental authority less repressive – an irre-
ducible core of top-down control and socialisation endures. Parents have power because they
are providers and their children dependants.
And they exercise that power in various ways,
sometimes to satisfy their own psychological
needs, sometimes in what they consider 'the
best interests' of their children, which tends to
mean encouraging or enforcing behaviour that
conforms to the imperatives of the social order.
Even the most liberal parents can hardly avoid
being the prototype of the teacher, the office
supervisor, and the police officer.

The small-household family can easily become claustrophobic and cloying, especially where one or more members is experiencing social and/or mental distress. Family members may become the butt of the anguish and rage of damaged psyches; they may be manipulated, moulded, remade to conform to the neurotic or psychotic needs of others; their own personalities – their confidence, autonomy, and identity – may degrade in a cauldron of family tension and animosity.

The dysfunctional character of many modern families was central to the work of radical psychiatrist R. D. Laing, discussed in books such as *The Divided Self* (1960), *The Self and Others* (1961), and *Sanity, Madness, and the Family* (1964). Laing considered 'chronic ontological insecurity' to be a modern social disease, one where individuals were threatened by 'engulfment', 'implosion', and 'petrification' in their relationships with others, causing them to become withdrawn, isolated, and lonely.

The self could only be authentic, could only realise itself, through engagement with others in society; but, argued Laing, while the psychotic longed for complete union, 'of this very longing he is terrified, because it will be the end of his self'. Other people, instead of being loved, become hated, because they are threatening, disabling, suffocating, liable to consume the self to satisfy their own febrile needs. Madness, for Laing, was always a matter of failed relationships with other people.

Laing published a series of case-studies based on his own practice at London's Tavistock Clinic. He revealed how parents would project onto each other and onto their children their own neurotic/psychotic needs. His conclusion was that the modern liberal family could be as dysfunctional as the traditional patriarchal family; different of course, but perhaps as liable to lead to mental illness. 'Our impression,' he concluded, 'comparing the families of schizophrenics with other families, is that they are relatively closed systems, and that the future patient is particularly enclosed within the family system.' In other words, a 'close family' – if by that we mean one that is inward-looking and exclusionary – is liable to be an incubator of mental illness.

Particularly significant is a modern form of parenting that places exceptional emphasis on approved forms of personal behaviour and achievement, where parents have internalised the competitive ethos of neoliberal capitalism and then project it onto their children. Psychologist Oliver James, in *The Selfish Capitalist* (2008), discusses the way in which this kind of 'cold, conditional, controlling parenting' fosters emotional distress and mental illness; more precisely, it fosters narcissism.

5

The narcissistic-authoritarian personality

Shakespeare's *Othello* is a study in psychosis. For those who do not know the play, here is the basic plot. Though a Moor – a man of North African origin – Othello is an accomplished military commander in the service of Renaissance Venice. At the beginning of the play, he is self-assured, proud of his achievements, certain of his position in the world; so much so in fact that, depending on how the role is played, his apparent lack of emotion can seem somewhat chilling. His factotum, Iago, a man he trusts unquestioningly, though openly subservient, is consumed with envy and resentment, hates his master, and plots his downfall. Iago insinuates that Desdemona, Othello's much-loved wife, is unfaithful.

Iago succeeds in tapping deep-rooted insecurity and anxiety, and thereby triggers a paranoid reaction. Othello, the puffed-up, boastful warlord, is transformed into a raging patriarchal misogynist who abuses his blameless and devoted wife, publicly humiliating and assaulting her, and finally, with careful premeditation and in cold blood, murdering her.

Terry Eagleton, writing in his *William Shakespeare* (1986), says of Othello that he was 'a man in hot pursuit of nothing'. (And I should say that I owe my reading of *Othello* to Eagleton's insights.) The murder of Desdemona is the act of a psychopath; more precisely, the act of a narcissistic-authoritarian paranoiac.

What might be called 'the Othello complex' is the primary personality disorder of our time. I put equal emphasis on both elements – narcissism and authoritarianism – and I see these as psychotic regressions, a flight from freedom, from other people, from human creativity and cooperation, to a dark world of loneliness, anxiety, imagined threats, and violent rages, one fostered by exceptional levels of atomisation, alienation, and anomie. The rest of this chapter is an attempt to explain, substantiate, and illustrate this claim.

Narcissism

What is narcissism? It is a neurotic-psychotic retreat from others, from society, from union; it is a withdrawal of self from engagement with the external world; it is a regression to a more infantile stage in libido development. Recall that Freud talked about the oral-cannibalistic and anal-sadistic stages, both characterised by auto-erotism, where the infant is focused on sensual pleasure by means of its own body. Here is Fromm's succinct summation of infant narcissism:

> The infant, at the moment of birth, would feel the fear of dying, if a gracious fate did not preserve it from any awareness of the anxiety involved in separation from the mother, and from intra-uterine existence. Even after being

born, the infant is hardly different from what it was before birth; it cannot recognise objects, it is not yet aware of itself, and of the world as being outside itself. It only feels the positive stimulation of warmth and food, and it does not yet differentiate warmth and food from its source: mother. Mother is warmth, mother is food, mother is the euphoric state of satisfaction and security. This state is one of narcissism, to use Freud's term. The outside reality, persons and things, have meaning only in terms of their satisfying or frustrating the inner state of the body. Real is only what is within; what is outside is real only in terms of my needs – never in terms of its own qualities or needs.

Store this picture in your mind, for you will find this primal narcissism echoed in the dysfunctional behaviour of so many adults, past and present. One is immediately reminded of historical tyrants like Alexander the Great, of interwar fascist leaders like Mussolini and Hitler, and of contemporary authoritarian-right politicians like Trump, Bolsonaro, and Johnson.

Let us recall also Freud's insistence that each stage in infantile libido development is imprinted on the psyche, creating a layer cake of hidden impulses and wishes. Repression and sublimation aim to bring these impulses and wishes into conformity with the demands of everyday life, but these processes are liable to malfunction, especially in the cauldron of many small-household families.

Nor is character fixed. Within quite broad parameters, character may change in response to changing social circumstances. On the one hand, atomisation, alienation, and anomie, compounded by the general stresses of social life in an exploitative class society, can cause implosion, regression, and the onset of mental illness. On the other, involvement in activism and struggle can become a journey in solidarity, self-discovery, and self-realisation (more on this in the final chapter).

So narcissistic tendencies can develop in childhood and/or be engendered by later social experience. And as soon as we think about the culture of modern neoliberal capitalism, we realise that almost everything about it discourages healthy, out-going, affirmative relationships with others and instead fosters narcissistic withdrawal.

We have used the Marxist concept of alienation to analyse this culture. We have defined our species-being in terms of free, creative, collective labour; as involving a practical relationship with nature, society, and the material world; as requir-ing us to be active makers of our own culture – artisans, artists, scientists, and scholars. We have contrasted this with contemporary human experi-ence under the rule of capital, where there is multi-layered alienation, an inner hollowness, a deep unhappiness, because we are estranged from na-ture and the land, from free association with our fellows, from the productive process, from our real needs, from materiality itself, from our real selves.

Let us review the social forces feeding narcis-sism in more detail. First, we are required to sell ourselves on the labour market, to commodify our personalities, to wear a mask of cheerful confor-mity to please the boss, the manager, the supervi-sor. The mask can become such a fixture that the real self dissolves into it, as we internalise the corporate-bureaucratic ethos, becoming mere person-ifications of an oppressive social order, cogs in the capitalist machine, automatons like Huxley's Be-tas, Gammas, Deltas, and Epsilons.

Then we are encouraged to assert a fake indi-viduality; not a real individuality based on activity and achievement, but another kind of mask, one designed by corporate advertising and social media, one formed of consumer bric-a-brac. We are en-couraged to adopt 'identities'; again, not real iden-tities formed organically by an engagement of self with others, but off-the-peg ersatz identities that find their expression in consumption and display.

As well as alienated labour and alienated con-sumerism, there is, too, a pervasive alienation in what is supposed to be 'free time' – the gorging on game shows, soap operas, and reality TV; the ob-sessive-compulsive addiction to social media; the hoovering up of celebrity tittle-tattle; the trawling of corporate marketing and manic online shop-ping; the pursuit of sex devoid of love or friend-ship; the bingeing on drugs, alcohol, and fast-food; and so much more. Passivity, lethargy, and empti-ness underlie the glitz and bustle, the hectic hedonism, the sensation-seeking, the instant gratification.

This modern condition is explored by psychologist Oliver James in his best-selling *Affluenza* (2007) and *The Selfish Capitalist* (2008). Finding that the incidence of mental illness (or what he calls 'emotional distress') has increased dramatically since the 1970s, and that it is now exceptionally high in the English-speaking developed world, James argues that neoliberal capitalism, personal insecurity, and competitive individualism are at the root of the problem.

Making copious reference to Fromm's *The Sane Society* (1956), but drawing heavily on more recent empirical research, James develops the concept of 'materialism', which he defines as preoccupation with 'money, possessions, appearances, and fame'. This is as good an angle of view us any. Joining the dots, James writes of a 'materialism-misery correlation'. 'Materialists,' he writes,

are more emotionally insecure, have poorer quality personal relationships, are more inauthentic and lacking in a sense of autonomy, and have lower self-esteem. They watch more television, and the kind of programmes they tend to prefer make them more materialistic. As children they are likely to have parents who make love conditional on performance and are obsessed with results at school, making their offspring materialistic...

... a person whose fundamental practical needs are met, as is the case for most of the citizens in the developed world, but who is still highly materialistic, is engaged in relative materialism: in essence, they want the money, possessions, appearances, or fame in order to keep up with the Joneses.

The materialist rejects as libidinally and socially positive attitudes such generosity, helpfulness, forgiveness, loyalty, solidarity and so on; these are viewed cynically as signs of weakness and gullibility. What is happening here is that the libido is in retreat, turning in on itself, regressing to a corrosive narcissism.

Popular understanding imagines narcissism to mean self-love. It means the opposite: it means self-hatred. The boredom, lack of feeling, and dull emptiness of modern life leaves, as Christopher Lasch describes it in *The Culture of Narcissism* (1979), 'a void within'.

Modern Americans, Lasch argues, are 'outwardly bland, submissive, and sociable', but inside 'they seethe with an inner anger'. Success degenerates into compulsive money-making and competitive display, mere appearance, form without substance. Inside, the futility gnaws at the soul. The social order thereby encourages 'a form of self-absorption' in which 'archaic elements increasingly dominate the personality structure and the self shrinks back'.

It shrinks to a place where people are 'tortured by self-consciousness', where they struggle 'to find meaning and purpose in life, to find something to live for'. But in fact they find nothing, for there is only a dull, draining, debilitating fixation on self, an inability to achieve cathexis in love and labour, in outward-directed, object-oriented, self-realising relationships with others.

'Modern selfishness,' wrote Erich Fromm in *Fear of Freedom* (1941/42),

> is the greed that is rooted in the frustration of the real self and whose object is the social self. While modern man seems to be characterised by utmost assertion of the self, actually he has been weakened and reduced to a segment of the total self ... to the exclusion of all other parts of the total personality.

The narcissistic personality is not only hollow, but also insecure, lacking in confidence, and low in self-esteem. Relationships with others involve, on the one hand, dependence and submission, for the weakened self, the regressive psyche, needs propping up; on they other, they involve envy, resentment, hostility, especially towards those better able to assert their freedom and creativity. It is for this reason that the narcissist – in flight from freedom – is also an authoritarian.

Authoritarianism

Infantile narcissism is associated with masochism and sadism. The infant craves physical intimacy, wants to be embraced by warmth and affection, finds in it a womb-like sensuality and security. But it also harbours feelings of anger and rage, it can be aggressive and violent, biting on the nipple, banging with its fists, kicking its legs in frustration.

The imprint is indelible. It is the root of masochism and sadism – two closely related complexes, one essentially a desire to be dominated, the other a desire to dominate, both arising from what Laing called 'chronic ontological insecurity'. Here is how Fromm explains it:

> The masochistic person escapes from the unbearable feeling of isolation and separateness by making himself part and parcel of another person who directs him, guides him, protects him; who is his life and oxygen, as it were. The power of the one to whom he submits is inflated, may he be a person or a god; he is every-

thing, I am nothing, except inasmuch as I am part of him. As a part, I am part of greatness, of power, of certainty. The masochistic person does not have to make decisions, does not have to take any risks. He is never alone, but he is not independent; he has no integrity; he is not yet fully born.

On the other hand:

The sadistic person wants to escape from his aloneness and his sense of imprisonment by making another person part and parcel of himself. He inflates and enhances himself by incorporating another person, who worships him. The sadistic person is as dependent on the submissive person as the latter is on the former; neither can live without the other. The difference is only that the sadistic person commands, exploits, hurts, humiliates, and that the masochistic person is commanded, exploited, hurt, humiliated...

This is a considerable difference in a realistic sense; in a deeper emotional sense, the difference is not as great as that which they both have in common: fusion without integrity. If one understands this, it is also not surprising to find that usually a person reacts in both the sadistic and masochistic manner, usually towards different objects.

This contradictory unity of masochism and sadism, rooted in ontological insecurity, inextricably associated with narcissism, brings us to the very heart of our conception of the mass psychology of fascism. 'This dichotomy – submission to powers above and domination over those below – is characteristic of the authoritarian character,' explains Fromm. Or again: 'Love for authority and hatred against those who are powerless are typical traits of authoritarian character.'

This is easy to understand. The narcissistic personality suffers from acute anxiety and experiences the social world not as something life-affirming, but as something threatening, liable to undermine a timid, fragile, regressive self.

That anxiety is damned-up libido seeking release. Incapable of finding fulfilment in love and labour, in effective and affective connection with others, it seeks release in a perverse kind of union, the only kind open to it, where the narcissistic personality seeks security in controlling, dominating, oppressive relationships. Narcissism and authoritarianism are twins.

But authoritarianism cannot fill the inner emptiness. The damaged psyche remains insecure and lonely, dependent on authority, in flight from freedom, fearful of others. Chronic anxiety continues to gnaw at the innards. The self feels exposed, vulnerable, liable to shatter. That is why it can explode into rage.

This rage is psychotic. It is not a rational rage triggered by real dangers in a social world correctly apprised. It is an irrational rage founded on an alternative construct of imagined threats. It is fascist rage.

What is fascism? We have defined it as the hyper-charging of a reactionary cocktail of ideas –

nationalism, racism, misogyny, homophobia, authoritarianism, militarism – so as to create an active political force opposed to progressive movements and radical change. That reactionary cocktail is rooted in irrationalism – in an appeal to tradition, to the fantasies of blood-and-soil nationalism, to a bundle of fables, prejudices, and icons handed down from the past. It is a throwback to pre-Enlightenment, pre-scientific ways of thinking; it is the myths of the 11th century broadcast by the technology of the 21st. It summons forces from the ideological sewers of capitalist society and the psychic sewers of the human unconscious. Formed of atomised, alienated, anomic humanity, spewing what Marx called 'the shit of ages', bloated with psychotic rage, fascism is the mechanism by which a deeply dysfunctional, crisis-ridden system of exploitation and oppression seeks to smash democracy, civil liberties, and any effective resistance to the rule of the rich and the corporations.

Newspeak

In 1930s Germany, the automatons of totalitarianism were indoctrinated by newspapers, radio, and cinema. From these crude media of party/state propaganda, they learned that they were a global master-race of supermen, but one threatened by race mixing and cultural extinction, by an international Jewish conspiracy that extended from Moscow to Wall Street, and by hordes of Slavic sub-men fit only for conquest and enslavement.

Today, fascist irrationalism has acquired an infinitely more powerful communications network, and a ready audience of billions of alienated addicts.

The science of semiotics is relevant here. Semiotics concerns the relationship between signs/symbols, above all language, and the real world. Central to it is the gap between the *signifier* (sign/symbol) and the *signified* (that which it refers to). Even a simple concrete noun like 'dog' turns out to be an abstraction, for the term is a generic species classification of biological science whose application to any particular animal involves a theoretical leap. Matters became infinitely more complex in the case of common abstract nouns like 'democracy', 'art', or 'truth'.

The socialist writer George Orwell – a master of the English language and an impassioned champion of truthful discourse – explored the political implications in different ways in his three greatest works. Serving in the POUM militia in the Spanish Civil War, he experienced first-hand the Stalinist-led counter-revolution which destroyed the workers' and peasants' revolutionary movement in 1937. His memoir, *Homage to Catalonia* (1938), records his experience and his embittered reaction to the international campaign of lying which had smothered the truth of what had happened.

He later wrote the satirical fantasy novella *Animal Farm* (1945), which charts the destruction of a popular revolution from within by a new bureaucratic ruling class, followed by the full-length novel *Nineteen Eighty-Four* (1949), which describes a bleak near-future dystopia of totalitarian dictatorship, mass surveillance, and relentless indoctrination.

In *Nineteen Eighty-Four*, the relationship between *signifier* and *signified* breaks down completely with the development of 'Newspeak', where language is turned inside out as words perform somersaults and reverse their meaning – peace becomes war, democracy becomes dictatorship, freedom becomes slavery, and so on. Words that can reverse their meaning cease to have any meaning, of course, making thought itself, certainly any kind of critical thought, impossible.

The automatons who support the authoritarian right are of this kind. They have effectively ceased to think as independent human-beings. They are like the loud-mouthed loyalist in the works canteen described by Orwell in *Nineteenth Eighty-Four*:

... though you could not actually hear what the man was saying, you could not be in any doubt about its general nature. He might be denouncing Goldstein [a thinly disguised Trotsky] and demanding sterner measures against thought-criminals and saboteurs, he might be fulminating against the atrocities of the Eurasian army, he might be praising Big

Brother or the heroes on the Malabar front – it made no difference. Whatever it was, you could be certain that every word of it was pure orthodoxy ... Winston had the curious feeling that this was not a real human-being but some kind of dummy. It was not the man's brain that was speaking, it was his larynx. The stuff that was coming out of him consisted of words, but it was not speech in the true sense: it was a noise uttered in unconsciousness, like the quacking of a duck.

In Orwell's imaginary totalitarian state, both surveillance and indoctrination are performed by telescreens on the wall of every living-room. This is familiar now. Screens, electronic images, and disconnected data dominate our lives.

In the virtual world of digitalised communication, the *signifier* is completely detached from the *signified*, has no anchoring in anything real, is beyond the essential test of practical activity in material existence. Online, anything can be true, anything false. In cyberspace, science, reason, and truth dissolve into trillions of pixels.

Here are some measures of the digitalised madness. More than half of Republican voters in the US believe that the result of the 2020 presidential election was fraudulent, and almost as many believe the storming of the Capitol in an attempt to stop ratification was justified. Around 60% of Republicans believe at least some of the claims of online QAnon conspiracy theory, about 40% are opposed to Covid vaccination, and as few as 30% believe the scientific evidence for global warming.

When people who voted Leave in Britain's Brexit referendum were polled, researchers found that 90% thought immigration was bad for the economy, 80% were opposed to equal opportunities for women and LGBTQI+ people, and 75% wanted longer prison sentences and restoration of the death penalty. Two-thirds of Leave voters in 2016 then went on to vote Tory in the 2019 general election.

Among Tory Party members, more than a third consider terrorist attacks to reflect widespread hostility to Britain in the Muslim community, almost half rate Islam 'a threat to the British way of life', and well over half believe 'there are no-go areas in Britain where sharia law dominates and non-Muslims cannot enter'. Boris Johnson, the leader of their party, has called gay men 'tank-topped bumboys', Muslim women 'letterboxes', and black people 'piccaninnies' with 'watermelon smiles'.

The rise and rise of the authoritarian right is powered by a collapse in rational, critical, evidence-based thought; and that in turn is rooted in a pandemic of extreme narcissistic individualism fostered by neoliberal capitalism.

6

Fascism and revolution

In *Macbeth*, the tragedy unfolds inside the leading protagonists' heads; the essence of the play is the psychic implosion of the *égoïsme à deux*, Macbeth and Lady Macbeth, whose personalities disintegrate under an unbearable burden of guilt. In *King Lear*, the conflict plays out between two sets of characters, one representing Virtue and Love (Lear, Cordelia, Kent, Edgar, Gloucester, Albany, the Fool), the other Evil and Hate (Goneril, Regan, Edmund, Cornwall, Oswald).

The latter are cold and callous. They are self-ishness personified. They are likened in the play to wild animals, to adders, wolves, tigers, and 'monsters of the deep'. Nature is convulsed by storms as

we see humanity 'reeling back into the beast', de-
vouring itself, descending into 'very Night herself'.

Yet against this we must set the honesty, de-
votion, and compassion, the nobility of soul, of
the virtuous; above all, that of the old king, who,
puffed up by the flattery of court sycophants, had
grown haughty in his pomp and power, and
thereby rendered foolish and blind, becoming the
instrument of his own destruction. The play charts
the redemption of Lear – the dawning of wisdom
in late old age – through the experience of des-
titution and insanity. He comes not only to consciousness of his own folly and of the evil he has
unleashed, but also to compassion for society's vic-
tims, the poor, the homeless, and the outcast.

The evil depicted in Shakespeare is the evil pro-
moted by capitalism, the Tories, and the authoritarian right. It is rooted in ambition, greed, and
selfishness; in a grasping, ruthless, anti-social individualism. It shatters the social and moral order,
reducing everything to a war of all against all, devoid of empathy, compassion, and solidarity. It cre-
ates a dystopian anarchy of human beastliness.

Set this humanist vision against the Tory record

of 'social murder' (a term coined by Frederick Engels in 1845 to describe the mass atrocities of the ruling class). The deaths in ambulances because of Tory NHS cuts. The suicides of disabled people because of Tory benefit cuts. The mass murder in Yemen because of Tory-supplied armaments. The Covid fatalities because of Tory pandemic negligence. The drownings in the Channel because of Tory border controls.

We live in an increasingly polarised world. On one side stand capital, the state, the authoritarian right, and the fascists. They at once foster and feed off a pandemic of extreme narcissistic individualism rooted in atomisation, alienation, and anomie. They direct psychotic rage against scapegoats, against the poor and powerless, against the exploited and oppressed, against the wretched of the earth. They are Shakespeare's beasts.

On the other side stand the progressives. Whatever their overt politics – liberal, social-democratic, radical, revolutionary – they are imbued with social responsibility, they empathise with others, they think in terms of humanity and the planet, they support reforms that will succour the needy, they are prepared to protest injustice, oppression, and violence.

Fromm explores these contrasting mindsets in *The Art of Loving* (1956/57). He counterposes the regressive, sado-masochistic, narcissistic-authoritarian personality with a healthy, mature, outward-directed, socially engaged personality. The latter is based not only on the projection of love/libido onto others, but also on love taking the primary form of giving, and giving generically and, as it were, instinctively. As Fromm puts it:

Love is not primarily a relationship to a specific person; it is an attitude, an orientation of character which determines the relatedness of a person to the world as a whole, not towards one 'object' of love. If a person loves only one other person and is indifferent to the rest of his fellow men, his love is not love but a symbiotic attachment, or an enlarged egotism... love is an activity, a power of the soul ... If I truly love one person, I love all persons, I love the world, I love life. If I can say to somebody else, 'I love you,' I must be able to say, 'I love in you every-body, I love through you the world, I love in you also myself.'

This turns the popular misconception of nar-cissism on its head. Narcissism means selfishness and social withdrawal; it means psychic separation and loneliness, and therefore inner emptiness; it is rooted in insecurity, low self-esteem, and lack of confidence; deep down, it is a gnawing sense of inadequacy, failure, and self-hate that gives rise to envy, resentment, and rage.

Fromm contrasts sexual relationships based upon healthy libido with those characterised by alienation, narcissism, and instrumentality, the *egoïsme à deux* so characteristic of neoliberal soci-ety, where there is a desperate clinging together of damaged psyches in flight from loneliness. 'Love,' he writes,

Love as mutual sexual satisfaction, and love as 'teamwork' and as a haven from aloneness, are the two 'normal' forms of the disintegration of love in modern Western society, the socially patterned pathology of love.

Fromm locates this 'pathology of love' firmly within the framework of Marx's conception of alienation. It is partly for this reason that he is able to say that those who truly love others – who project libido onto partners, family, friends, colleagues, the oppressed, the whole of suffering humanity – must, necessarily, also love themselves; that is to say, in effect, they are happy and fulfilled. 'Care, responsibility, respect, and knowledge,' he tell us,

Care, responsibility, respect, and knowledge are mutually interdependent. They are a syndrome of attitudes which are to be found in the mature person; that is, in the person who develops his own powers productively, who only wants to have that which he has worked for, who has given up narcissistic dreams of omniscience and omnipotence, who has acquired humility based on the inner strength which only genuine productive activity can give.

A polarised world

Social and political polarisation, therefore, has its psychological correlate. In the United States, in the 2020 presidential election, 81 million Americans voted Democrat and 74 million Republican. In Britain, in the 2016 EU referendum, 48% voted Remain and 52% Leave, and in the 2019 general election, a narrow majority voted for centre and left-of-centre parties (Labour, Lib Dems, Greens, SNP, Plaid Cymru, and Sinn Féin) and 44% Tory. In Brazil, in the 2018 presidential election, 44% voted for the Workers Party candidate and 55% for Jair Bolsonaro.

Further examples could be given. In each case, what is represented, in the crude arithmetic of electoral politics, is polarisation between a progressive bloc of voters and a reactionary bloc prepared to vote for the authoritarian right – to vote, that is, against their own freedom and for their own servitude.

We have already noted the results of opinion poll surveys that have confirmed the depth of reactionary sentiment. Right-wing voters register strong support for nationalism, racism, sexism, homophobia, militarism, police power, conspiracy theory, climate-change denial, and so on. My argument here is that this political advance of the authoritarian right is rooted in a generic personality disorder – extreme narcissistic individualism – fostered by the exceptional levels of atomisation, alienation, and anomie characteristic of neoliberal capitalist society.

But I have also argued that healthy libidinal development and mature, positive, outward-going personalities form the basis of progressive politics and mass movements of resistance. Not only that, but these opposing social, political, and psychological forces are not in any way static entities. We can posit the existence, at one pole, of a minority of committed radicals, and at the other, a minority of hardened fascists. But we can assume that the majority lie somewhere on the spectrum in-between, their affiliations, indeed their very personalities, able to change.

People are naturally greedy and selfish, so things will never change. How often have you heard this argument against socialism? It is the argument of cynics and pessimists who have given up on life; and it is wilfully ignorant.

We have examples all around us of generous, open-hearted behaviour; of empathy, compassion, and solidarity; of human interactions that reflect our species-being as social animals defined by co-operation, collective labour, and the creation of shared culture and wellbeing. It would be pointless to quote examples: every reader will be able to think of their own, both from their own experience and from their knowledge of society as a whole.

Were human society governed by greed and self-ishness, a war of all against all, we would never have left the Stone Age. Every stage in human social and cultural development has depended upon cooperation and sharing. For tens of thousands of years, we have worked together to hunt, to herd animals, to till the soil, to share meals, to make clothes, to build homes, to educate our children, to look after the sick, to provide for the needy. Whereas selfish individualism, riding rough-shod over the social good, the moral order, is, as Shakespeare knew, the very essence of evil.

So how do we change people so we can change the world? How do we lift people from an alienated, privatised, narcissistic, miserable existence where they are prey to the reactionary ideas of the authoritarian right to a new way of being where they are outgoing, proactive, socially engaged, and politically committed?

Marx had an answer to this question. He was writing before there was a scientific psychology – psychoanalysis – but he was nonetheless an exceptionally astute observer of mass consciousness. Drawing on Hegelian philosophy, the dialectical idea that the social world is a contradictory unity in motion, where nothing is fixed and fast-frozen, where everything is in flux, in a permanent state of becoming, he argued that people change in the act of changing the world.

This is confirmed by every mass struggle from below. Whenever the working class, the oppressed, and the poor begin to organise themselves to fight for change, they gain in confidence and consciousness. Confidence comes from uniting with others, from overcoming alienation and isolation, from discovering there is fellowship and strength in collective action. Consciousness comes from the effect of action on the social world. Talk changes nothing. First is the deed. To act is to provoke a response in others, to begin a social interaction, a coming together of progressive forces on one side, a counter-mobilisation of reaction on the other – for we live in a class society, where decent people will instinctively support those fighting injustice, while capital and the state will move to crush resistance.

When Tory Prime Minister Margaret Thatcher set out to shut down the coal industry, crush the miners' union, and destroy the livelihoods of hundreds of thousands of people in 1984, the miners, their families, and their supporters fought back. So Thatcher sent in the police to smash up the picket lines, escort scabs into the pits, and arrest strike leaders.

What a lesson? On the one hand, there was the

exhilarating solidarity of the mass meetings, the strike canteens, the picket lines, the pitched battles with the police; there was a sense of the tremendous power and nobility of working people when they stand and fight together. On the other, there was the discovery that the government, the state, the police, and the media were not neutral, but class enemies, a nexus of power representing the interests of big business and the rich. So thousands of miners and their families were radicalised by the experience of the year-long strike.

Women were perhaps even more radicalised than men. The miners themselves were already staunch trade unionists with a long tradition of militant struggle behind them. The women of the mining communities were often housewives or perhaps part-time workers without union experience. Yet thousands of them became actively involved in the strike, not only in 'traditional' roles like running strike canteens, but joining the picket lines, organising demonstrations, raising money, speaking at meetings, producing leaflets, making banners, and so on. They eventually formed Women Against Pit Closures at a delegate conference held in Chesterfield in December 1984. They were inspired by both the strike itself and the feminist movement. They were a clear example of what Marx meant when he wrote that working people change themselves when they act to change the world.

It is the class struggle itself that offers hope. To end the mental anguish of life under capitalism – to destroy the social conditions that give rise to narcissism, authoritarianism, and the mass psychology of fascism – we must transcend alienation by restoring the commons to the people, by establishing democratic control over economic and social life, and by healing the metabolic rupture between nature and society. We must create a world in which love and labour can flourish in new communities based on cooperation, solidarity, and freedom. But in the struggle to get there – in the struggle against injustice here and now, and in the struggle for red-green revolution and a world transformed in the long run – we can begin the process of overcoming our alienation from each other and the process of restoring social balance and mental health.

It is necessary to mobilise millions. To do this, we must show there is an alternative. This requires both a vision of a different world based on democracy, equality, peace, and sustainability, and also the example of action in fighting for such a world. Ideas and struggle. Theory and practice. If we do this right, we can lift others from their privatised misery, from their subservience to capital and the state, and re-energise them in new communities of solidarity and struggle.

Trotsky, writing in the 1930s, described fascism as the counter-revolutionary movement of despair and socialism as the revolutionary movement of hope. So it is today. We might add that fascism is also the movement of narcissism and authoritarianism, of selfishness and the cult of the bully, while socialism is the movement of love and labour, of solidarity and cooperation, of mature, healthy, outgoing libido. Or, as Wilhelm Reich put it, 'Love, work, and knowledge are the wellsprings of our life. They should also govern it.'

A few months before he was murdered by a Stalinist agent, Trotsky wrote a short testament to be published after his death. It ended with these words: 'Life is beautiful. Let the future generations cleanse it of all evil, oppression, and violence, and enjoy it to the full.'

That is now our task if we are to save ourselves from ourselves in the global crisis of the early 21st century.

Abraham, Karl, 1942, *Selected Papers on Psycho-analysis*, London, Hogarth Press.

Adorno, T W *et al*, 1950, *The Authoritarian Personality*, New York, Harper & Row.

Bowlby, John, 1953, *Child Care and the Growth of Love*, Harmondsworth, Penguin.

Bradley, A. C., 1904, *Shakespearean Tragedy: lectures on Hamlet, Othello, King Lear, and Macbeth*, London, Macmillan & Co.

Brown, Norman, O., 1959, *Life Against Death: the psychoanalytical meaning of history*, London, Sphere Books.

Browning, Christopher, R., 1992, *Ordinary Men: Reserve Police Battalion 101 and the Final Solution in Poland*, London, HarperCollins.

Debord, Guy, 1967/1994, *The Society of the Spectacle*, New York, Zone Books.

Deleuze, Gilles and Guattari, Félix, 1972/2013, *Anti-Oedipus: capitalism and schizophrenia*, London, Bloomsbury.

Eagleton, Terry, 1986, *William Shakespeare*, Oxford, Blackwell.

Engels, Frederick, 1845, *The Condition of the Working Class in England*, at www.marxists.org

Faulkner, Neil, with Samir Dathi, 2017, *Creeping Fascism: Brexit, Trump, and the Rise of the Far Right* (1st ed.), London, Public Reading Rooms.

Faulkner, Neil, with Samir Dathi, Phil Hearse, and Seema Syeda, 2019, *Creeping Fascism: what it is and how to fight it* (2nd ed.), London, Public Reading Rooms.

Faulkner, Neil, Hearse, Phil, Fortune, Nina, Fortune, Rowan, and Hannah, Simon, 2021, *System Crash: an activist guide to making revolution*, London/Amsterdam, Resistance Books/International Institute for Research and Education.

Faulkner, Neil, 2021, *Alienation, Spectacle, and Revolution: a critical Marxist essay*, London, Resistance Books.

Ferenczi, Sandor, 1923/1968, *Thalassa: a theory of genitality*, New York, W. W. Norton & Co.

Freud, Sigmund, 1899/1976, *The Interpretation of Dreams*, Pelican Freud Library, Vol 4, Harmondsworth, Penguin.

Freud, Sigmund, 1905/1977, *On Sexuality: three essays on the theory of sexuality and other works*, Pelican Freud Library, Vol 7, Harmondsworth, Penguin.

Fromm, Erich, 1941/1942, *The Fear of Freedom*, London, Routledge & Kegan Paul.

Fromm, Erich, 1956, The Sane Society, London, Routledge & Kegan Paul.

Fromm, Erich, 1956/1957, *The Art of Loving*, London, George Allen & Unwin.

Fisher, Mark, 2009, *Capitalist Realism: is there no alternative?* Alresford, Zero Books.

Goffman, Erving, 1959, *The Presentation of Self in Everyday Life*, New York, Anchor Books.

Horney, Karen, 1937, *The Neurotic Personality of Our Time*, New York, W. W. Norton & Co.

Horney, Karen, 1939, *New Ways in Psychoanalysis*, New York, W. W. Norton & Co.

Huxley, Aldous, 1932, *Brave New World*, London, Chatto & Windus.

James, Oliver, 2008, *The Selfish Capitalist: the origins of affluenza*, London, Vermilion.

Laing, R. D., 1960, *The Divided Self: an existential*

study in sanity and madness, Harmondsworth, Penguin.

Laing, R. D., 1961, *The Self and Others*, London, Tavistock Publications.

Laing, R. D. and Esterson, Aaron, 1964, *Sanity, Madness, and the Family*, London, Penguin.

Lasch, Christopher, 1979, *The Culture of Narcissism: American life in an age of diminishing expectations*, New York, W. W. Norton & Co.

Marcuse, Herbert, 1955, *Eros and Civilisation: a philosophical enquiry into Freud*, Boston, Beacon Press.

Marcuse, Herbert, 1964, *One-Dimensional Man*, Boston, Beacon Press.

Marx, Karl, 1844, *Economic and Philosophical Manuscripts*, at www.marxists.org

Marx, Karl, 1848, *The Communist Manifesto*, at www.marxists.org

Marx, Karl, 1867, *Capital*, Vol 1, at www.marxists.org

Orwell, George, 1938, *Homage to Catalonia*, London, Secker & Warburg.

Orwell, George, 1945, *Animal Farm*, London, Secker & Warburg.

Orwell, George, 1949, *Nineteen Eighty-Four*, London, Secker & Warburg.

Rank, Otto, 1924/1952, *The Trauma of Birth*, New York, Robert Brunner.

Reich, Wilhelm, 1933/1975, *The Mass Psychology of Fascism*, Harmondsworth, Penguin.

Reich, Wilhelm, 1948/1975, *Listen, Little Man!* Harmondsworth, Penguin.

Anti*Capitalist Resistance is an organisation of revolutionary socialists. We believe red-green revolution is necessary to meet the compound crisis of humanity and the planet.

We are internationalists, ecosocialists, and anticapitalist revolutionaries. We oppose imperialism, nationalism, and militarism, and all forms of discrimination, oppression, and bigotry. We support the self-organisation of women, Black people, disabled people, and LGBTQI+ people. We support all oppressed people fighting imperialism and forms of apartheid, and struggling for self-determination, including the people of Palestine.

We favour mass resistance to neoliberal capitalism. We work inside existing mass organisations, but we believe grassroots struggle to be the core of effective resistance, and that the emancipation of the working class and the oppressed will be the act of the working class and the oppressed ourselves.

We reject forms of left organisation that focus exclusively on electoralism and social-democratic reforms. We also oppose top-down 'democratic-centralist' models. We favour a pluralist organization that can learn from struggles at home and across the world.

We aim to build a united organisation, rooted in the struggles of the working class and the oppressed, and committed to debate, initiative, and self-activity. We are for social transformation, based on mass participatory democracy.

info@anticapitalistresistance.org
www.anticapitalistresistance.org

ABOUT RESISTANCE BOOKS

Resistance Books is a radical publisher of internationalist, ecosocialist, and feminist books. We publish books in collaboration with the International Institute for Research and Education in Amsterdam (www.iire.org) and the Fourth International (www.fourth.international/en). For further information, including a full list of titles available and how to order them, go to the Resistance Books website.

info@resistancebooks.org
www.resistancebooks.org

Lightning Source UK Ltd.
Milton Keynes UK
UKHW020010030622
403923UK00012B/206

9 780902 869318